LET IT BEGIN WITH ME

CHRIS THOMAS

First published in 2017 by
New Life Publishing, Luton,
Bedfordshire LU4 9HG

© Chris Thomas

British Library Cataloguing in Publication Data
A catalogue record for this book is available
from the British Library

ISBN   978 1 912237 06 7

Unless otherwise stated Bible references are
from the New Jerusalem Bible, Darton, Longman
and Todd, UK (1985) and are used with permission.

Typesetting by New Life Publishing,
Luton, UK www.goodnewsbooks.co.uk
Printed and bound in Great Britain

LET IT BEGIN WITH ME

*...reflecting God's life
for the world*

CHRIS THOMAS

CONTENTS

In memory of my dad,
Chris, who gave me life.
His experiences and struggles
have made me the person I am
today and I thank God for him

ONE

THE NATURE OF GOD

Many years ago, when I was working in the prisons around Durham, I met a young man called Dean. He was on remand for having taken part in an armed robbery. He had pleaded guilty and was waiting to be sentenced. At first he was arrogant and cocky, saying to me that prison would be a breeze, and that he was not in the least bit afraid of what he had to face.

One day, I went in to the prison to see him and as soon as I walked in the door, I could see he was very distressed. His eyes were red from crying and his hands were shaking. His grandmother had died and he had been told that day. For the very first time the walls he had built up began to crumble. He told me that she had been very ashamed of what he had done and had not been able to face him since he went into prison. However she had sent him a card, in which she told him, that despite how she felt about what he had done, she still loved him and always would.

He then began to talk about the crime he had committed. He told me that he had always wanted to be part of something. At school he had been a loner having few friends. He had always felt on the outside and as though he did not belong anywhere. When he was about seventeen he began to get friendly with a group of young men who encouraged him to enter a life of petty crime. He experienced with them a sense of belonging and camaraderie. He felt included and respected by them.

Sadly the opposite was true. They had obviously seen in this sad and lonely young man someone who could be manipulated and used and eventually blamed for their crimes. They graduated to bigger crimes until the one he had been arrested for. As he sobbed and told me his story he said something I have never forgotten. He said in a very plaintive tone of voice, 'You know I just wanted to belong'.

That desire to belong somewhere seems to exist in every human being. Could it be this desire for unity has been planted in our hearts by God. More than that, could our desire for unity reflect the very nature of God who is one? Is that why in John's Gospel Jesus prays, 'Father may they be one'? So that the power of God might enable us to draw together much of the fragmentation that is in our lives and in the world and reveal the presence of God.

It seems to me that the desire for oneness and relationship has been planted in our hearts by God and that it reflects the reality of who God is, a God who is one, a God who is in perfect relationship. So what I would like to do in this opening chapter is to reflect on the nature of God and the revelation of God as perfect unity.

I love the Scriptures and reflecting on them and praying about them has become the bedrock of my life. When God found me, I was fifteen and this love of the Scriptures is the greatest gift I have been given, not least, because they have propelled me into the arena of transformation so often in my life.

If you go to the book of Genesis you will find in chapter 1 verse 26 this line, 'In the beginning the Lord, the God of Israel, says, 'Let us make humanity in our own image, in the likeness of ourselves'. I was reading somewhere recently that whoever wrote the book of Genesis was a mystic, someone who was entering into the revelation of who God is.

Without a huge amount of prayer and reflection it would be impossible to see God as perfect unity and yet the use of the words 'us' and 'ourselves' seems to imply that the author of Genesis has begun to recognise that God is more than a single being but rather a unity of persons.

Years of study reflection and dogmatic statements have recognised God as trinity but when you think the book of Genesis was written some five hundred years before the birth of Christ, it is quite extraordinary. The author or authors certainly had an insight into the reality of God. The word 'us' is God revealing Godself as community, as relationship itself. In the seminary we were taught that it was a procession of giving and receiving, both within God and outside of God. The word procession implies activity within the Godhead and activity which spills over into a creative burst of energy and becomes then, the pattern of all creation.

Richard Rohr says, 'Reality as communion became the template and pattern for our entire universe, from atoms to galaxies. The first philosophical problem of 'the one and the many' was already overcome in God; and we found ourselves to be both Monotheists and Trinitarians at the same time.'

We live in a universe of many diverse things; planets, stars, galaxies, all held in love with one another. When love becomes damaged and broken in any way, then the synchronisation of the universe is threatened. Is that not that what we are experiencing time and time again as people blow one another up?

Do the trouble spots in the world not threaten the

harmony of the whole world? As we milk the world for all we can get out of it, are we not causing immense damage to ecology and the natural order? When love is broken nothing works properly. There was a song released a few years ago called 'Where is the Love' by the Black Eyed Peas and one of the verses asks these questions: 'Whatever happened to the values of humanity? Whatever happened to the fairness and equality?' The verse goes on to say: 'Instead of spreading love we're spreading animosity. Lack of understanding, leading us away from unity.'

So God is the blue-print for perfect unity. Every aspect of creation is made to that blueprint, is created for harmony and all of the created order is connected. How sad that we destroy that harmony within ourselves and within the world.

It is as though we do not recognise that truth and yet every fibre of creation is screaming it out at us. Contemporary science seems to be aware of this unity of existence. Physicists, molecular biologists, astronomers, and other scientists recognise this universal pattern. Sadly it seems they recognise it much more easily than people of faith. They recognise that everything is connected and works together.

I came across a quotation from Teilhard de Chardin

who said: 'The physical structure of the universe is love.'
While that may be difficult to understand it has to be
true that if the unity within God is the blueprint for
the created order, and if God is love, then the universe
has to be based on love and of course it must be, if it
reveals the nature of God.

What does that mean for us? I think it means that we
have been given an invitation to recognise our call to
reveal this unity to the world. It is not clever words or
theological theses that reveal the pattern of all things
but the power of love. We show the reality of God to the
world by loving.

Dostoyevsky, in *The Brothers Karamazov,* wrote 'Love
people even in their sin, for that is the semblance of
Divine Love and is the highest love on earth. Love
all of God's creation, the whole and every grain of sand
of it. Love every leaf, every ray of God's light. Love
the animals, love the plants, love everything. If you
love everything, you will perceive the divine mystery
in things. Once you perceive it, you will begin to
comprehend it better every day. And you will come at
last to love the whole world with an all-embracing love.'

It is a way of saying two things. If you have fallen in
love with God then you will see the pattern of God
everywhere, in every person, in every leaf, in every

flower, in every tree. I find that so often when I talk to people who love God. They seem to have an innate sense that God is in all things. At times it is a struggle to find God in the most difficult of circumstances but there is a desire and a willingness to search and look for the presence of God everywhere.

The converse is also true of course. I was recently talking to a woman who comes to see me for spiritual accompaniment. She is a person of deep faith but she tells me that she came to faith by learning to love the world and everything in it. If you fall in love with the world then you cannot fail but discover God, who is the source and pattern for all creation. I think that is the second reality that Dostoyevsky teaches us.

Where does that call to love begin for us? I guess it is through experiencing God and in the experience of discovering that we are God's beloved children. My search for God began with an extraordinary experience of God finding me in the depths of my pain and hurt and telling me that I was special, beloved, and chosen. That experience was the starting point of a journey into the mystery of God that can never stop. There is always more to discover and the more I journey the more I know it is a journey into love.

I hope that the more I discover that everything is about

love then the more like love I become. I guess we have
to open ourselves up to love and surrender to it so that
we then naturally pass it on.

After that, everything we are and everything we do will
be about love. We will become the imitation of God.
The challenge is to see what God is doing all the time,
this creative, energising, unified being, and then do the
same thing. What we discover is that God can only love,
because it is the nature of God to love.

Just recently I was talking to ninety three year old
daughter of Charity, which is a Catholic religious order.
She was telling me that the happiest and most fulfilling
part of her day was when she spent an hour or so sitting
with God. She told me that she could not remember a
thing that happened during that time but she said, 'I
look at God and God looks at me and we laugh at each
other.'

I then asked her what was the most important lesson
she had learnt in the sixty plus years that she had been
a daughter of Charity. She told me that what she had
learnt, was to stay close to God, and in the staying close,
to let love form her. It was for me a very powerful image
of entering into the mystery that is God and revealing
that mystery that takes over every fibre of our being by
the way in which we love everything around us. This

sister was a wonderfully warm human being caught up in the mystery of God, love, and the universe.

It is a mystery that can consume us and invigorate us but a mystery we can never come to the end of. 'I look at God and God looks at me and we laugh at each other'.

So while we cannot understand the Godhead with our finite minds, we can experience and enter into relationship with that God. We can experience relationship with a creative God, a God who breathes life into the world and into us. The God in whom every creative thought and action has its origin is open to us and to relationship with us. This incredible creative power, the source of all that is, wants to know us and to love us and more than that, wants to continue creating within us and through us.

We can experience relationship with a saving God. Christian tradition tells us that Jesus is the God who saves. 'Saves us from what?' you might ask. Saves us, I think, from ourselves, if we only care to open ourselves to relationship with that God. God saves us from bitterness and anger and self-hatred and reveals the love that holds all things in being. This all powerful creative God, has become flesh in Jesus and through that becoming has opened the way to life that knows no end.

We can experience relationship with an indwelling God who leads us into the truth of relationship with God, of intimacy with God. That somehow the very essence of who God is comes to live within us. What is the key to experiencing and opening up to relationship? It seems to be time spent gazing at God and allowing God to gaze at us.

This relationship is not saying prayers, filling the space with empty words which make us feel good about having done our duty. It is not words meant to appease a God who demands, or so that we can get into heaven, or avoid hell. It is not about saying this novena or that novena in the hope that we can get God to change God's mind about certain things. It is simply being before God because God is God and because there is real life in God.

The invitation is to open ourselves to the reality of God and experience the life-giving presence of God who is life-giver, saviour and indweller. It is all about unity and becoming a mirror image of God who is love.

There are three words that capture some of my musings about the nature of God and which I think reveal to us what the love that underpins everything is all about. The words are strength, vulnerability and power.

Many years ago I watched an interview with Colin Parry who is the father of Tim, the young boy killed in the Warrington IRA bomb attack. It was a very poignant interview. Colin shared very deep emotions about his loss and his thoughts on the Northern Ireland situation and those who had planted the bomb that had murdered his son. Somehow, as I was watching, I knew that this man was never going to be destroyed by what had happened to him and his family.

More than his incredible bravery in the midst of terrible tragedy, Colin Parry helped me to crystallise something of my image of God in so far as you can ever capture in words something which is beyond words and in a sense can only be experienced.

As Colin Parry spoke and shared there was within him a strength, a vulnerability, and a power which, as I said, are three words which for me capture something of God.

In John's Gospel we are told that God so loved the world that he sent his son, not to condemn the world but so that through him, the world might be saved. For God to so love the world is about strength and vulnerability. The strength of a God whose desire is to create. The vulnerability of a God who would give up omnipotence and become a human being who suffered and died for love. When those two realities come together there is an explosion of power that is the Holy Spirit, which transforms and sets free.

Many years ago I was reading one of Richard Rohr's daily reflections. In it he described an image which has come to mean a lot to me when thinking about strength power and vulnerability. He described an ancient fresco or picture painted on the wall of a thirteenth century Lutheran Church. It has an image of an old man holding in his hands the orb of power. This is God the Father. On the opposite wall is the broken bleeding body of Jesus staring at the father with a look of such intensity and understanding and love that it almost breaks your heart. Then on the ceiling with rays of power coming from its wings is a dove symbolising the spirit. The relationship of pure love between the father and the son is the spirit, the power, which enables strength and vulnerability to be shared.

What does that say to us? Earlier in this chapter we reflected on the book of Genesis and particularly that we are made in the image and likeness of God. If that is true then within us there is the incredible strength of love. This strength enables us to choose to be vulnerable and to give ourselves away for the sake of the world. As that strength and vulnerability come together there is power, the power of love which first explodes into shape and form at the very beginning of time.

Those who challenge the world to recognise that love are those whose love is strong enough to let them give themselves away for the sake of the world. People like Martin Luther, Ghandi, Irene Sendler, Oscar Romero, Mother Teresa and countless unsung heroes.

The challenge for all of us, who are people of faith, is to find within ourselves the strength that comes from love and which is God. It is to discover love which does not count the cost and which is expressed through compassion and mercy and forgiveness. It is to find love, which has conquered the petty self-righteousness that so many of us live by and which forces us into that place of vulnerability. It is from that place, that for the sake of others we give our very lives away. It is in the doing and the living that we find power and reveal who God is.

I saw this very powerfully in the life of a young woman that I met some thirty five years ago. She had a revelation of the overwhelming love of God that is everywhere and in everything. The more she experienced that love, the more she felt called to share that love. Eventually Ann knew that the call of God was on her life and, having no dependants, she gave up her teaching job, sold her house, and followed the promptings of love. This led her to Africa where she began to build a school, believing that education could make a huge difference in people's lives.

Many of the children she began to educate were victims of Aids. Their parents had died and they lived on the streets, foraging for food, to all intents and purposes abandoned. Many of them became petty criminals or were sold into prostitution just to survive. So her next task was to build an orphanage. The children had to be got off the streets to live in a place of safety. This was followed by a clinic to treat those who were infected by the Aids virus and so the work has gone on for years and years with the support of a generous group of fundraisers. Anne's own money from the sale of her house has long since gone. Anne says there have been times when she has cried with the seeming hopelessness and enormity of the situation that she has chosen to live in. She weeps at the plight of the broken people she lives among and wonders at times if she can go on. Then, she said, a child looks at her with huge eyes full of tears and she sees the face of God and knows that she must carry on being love in order to reveal love.

A few years ago when I was a Parish Priest, our journey in faith group were touring around the Church looking at all the various elements we have and asking questions. It is always funny when someone asks you a question about something that you have always known or always seen because it makes you think about, and really look at, what it means for you.

We were walking around the Church and one of the women asked why when Catholics come into Church do they make the sign of the cross. It was something I had done all my life but I did not really have an answer for her. I mumbled something in response which seemed to satisfy her but which certainly did not satisfy me.

Since then I have though about it a lot and I have realised that for me it is a powerful reminder of the sort of relationship God wants with us. We are to live in the name of the father and of the Son and of the Holy Spirit and the Amen, which means 'Yes', is a commitment to that way of life.

In the book of Deuteronomy we are told that our God is alive. Every time we make the sign of the cross we affirm our faith in a God who is with us and is working in our lives, always leading us on and calling us to more life. We affirm our faith in love which is the very nature of God and which underpins the fabric of the universe.

The challenge of the sign of the cross is whether or not

that is the sort of God we believe in. Do we believe in the God who constantly calls us to newness and into the depths of love. Or do we believe in some dusty old concept that belongs on the top of a library shelf. Is God something, or someone, that we take down from that library shelf every Sunday, dust it off and then put back once we have been to Church? For many people that, sadly, is the case.

The God of the Scriptures is a dynamic reality not some fossilised entity preserved for posterity. We are invited to live in the life of the Trinity and through our witness to that life, others are to be invited to do the same. We are to be immersed in the life of the Trinity which is a life of love.

We are invited every day to be living in the compassionate love of the Father, enabled to believe in that love by the spirit and saved from those things that would stop us believing in love by the Son. It helps us to know that we are connected to the blueprint for the universe. That means of course, as we have tried to explore, that we are connected to every fibre of the universe that sustains us, the world we live in and every brother or sister who walks the earth. That knowledge is what brings the willingness to live life for the sake of the unity of love that underpins everything and to try and deal with anything that flies in the face of unity.

A few years ago a friend of mine asked me if I had read a book written by William Paul Young called *The Shack*. At the time I had not even heard of it but everywhere I went I found others talking about it and it seemed to divide opinion. People either loved or hated it. Eventually I bought a copy to see what the fuss was about. It was a book about God. It was about unity. It was about relationship. It was about harmony. I loved it! It has been questioned theologically, although I can see no reason to do that. It simply invites you into the mystery and to journey into God.

So if you do not quite grasp what I am trying to talk about in this chapter it might be worth getting a copy of *The Shack*. It says much of what I have been trying to explore in a very contemporary, creative, and dramatic way.

God is calling us for the sake of creation to see God everywhere and in everything. God is calling us to give our lives for the sake of relationship and unity. It could be the salvation of the world.

TWO

GOD IS LOVE

J
ust recently I was speaking at a conference and I met a man there who was a joy to be with. He was brimming with life and humour and I found myself wanting to be in his company. A few nights we had a drink together in the bar and he shared with me something of his journey. He talked of his search for more of God. He was never satisfied, always believing that he could journey further into the mystery that is God. He told me of his love for humanity and for the world we live in, a passionate, deep love that filled his being. He said that he had found God often in his life in his wife and children and grandchildren and in the unexpected meetings that set him alight within.

He told me that many years earlier he had cried out to God in desperation. His life had fallen apart. He had lost his job without a reference because he had been accused of fraud. His house was on the brink of being repossessed. He was drinking too much. His life was spiralling out of control.

He had been baptised and made his first holy communion but had not been to church since he was in his early teens. One day, he was passing a Church and before he knew it found himself inside crying. He said that as he cried his being was flooded with the most extraordinary feeling of love and he left that Church a different man. Problems did not just disappear, indeed they got worse for a while, but his attitude to them had changed. Unconditional love had made him a new creation. It was several years before he got back on his feet but he told me that every day he found himself thanking God for the gift of being loved and the difference that had made in his life.

We began by looking at God as a perfect unity of relationships. What I would like to do in this chapter is to reflect on how that God loves us. I know I have written and spoken about God's love many times over the years, but it seems to me vital that we allow the truth of love to make the journey from our heads to our guts. It is the knowledge of love for all, that will force us to give our lives for unity.

One of the marks of a Christian heart should be the desire for inclusivity, which leads to a desire to ultimately be in communion with the world and as many people as possible. The spirit of God enables you to move beyond demanding that other people become just like you before we can have communion. Sadly, we tend to harbour the opposite attitude, though we are slow to admit this and often are not prepared to. We are exclusive and push people away.

Most of us who say we are Christian, like to imagine that we are images of Jesus, or at least becoming images of him. After all disciples are to be like the master are they not? We all like to think of ourselves as having hearts that are big and all-encompassing. Most of us want to be deeply compassionate, suffering with people, walking alongside them. Love is the litmus test of Christianity and so we want to love as Jesus did but all too often our attitudes and our actions belie this. We are often far too focused on making ourselves right by proving others to be wrong.

Ronald Rolheiser says, 'Too often we have an unconscious mantra that says: I can only be good, if someone else is bad. I can only be right, if someone else is wrong. My dogma can only be true, if someone else's is false. My religion can only be right, if someone else's is wrong. My Eucharist can only be valid, if someone else's is invalid. And I can only be in heaven, if someone else is in hell.'

As Rolheiser says, most of the time we are not consciously aware that we are doing this. It is almost ingrained into us that we have to be dogmatically correct, which necessarily means somebody else is not.

Within our Catholic tradition we have to be the true Church which means that other communities are less than we are. We argue about correct liturgical practice looking down on those who see worship differently. It seems to be part of the ethos within Christianity that some people's morality is worse than ours. We cry out for justice when in fact we are looking for revenge and justify separating ourselves from those who are seen as bad and wrong. We divide and separate and judge and condemn.

While it is true that the scriptures and the tradition that has developed over the centuries are very clear about right and wrong, they are just as clear that the heart of God is open and loving towards all people. God's deep, constant, passionate longing is that every human being, regardless of how they live or what they do find a place in the heart of God. Again Rolheiser says, 'God, it seems, does not want to rest until everyone is home, eating at the same table.'

The reality of God's love is what will draw us together and help us to move beyond ourselves and look for unity with every human person and so this chapter is about the power that is love, filling us and drawing us beyond ourselves.

A few years ago I was working with a group of people

in Ireland. As part of the process people were given the opportunity to come and have a chat with me if they wanted to. All went well until one woman came in and said to me that she ran a house of prayer about fifteen miles from the place that we were working. I was told that in the House of Prayer was a weeping statue and that the statue wept every Wednesday and Friday. It seemed that about a hundred people gathered to see this phenomenon.

Anyone who knows me will know that this sort of thing is not my scene and so I gently steered the conversation away from the weeping statue and on to other things. The next day she came back and again started to talk about her weeping statue. She asked for prayer and the prayer was that the statue would weep on a Tuesday and a Thursday as well as the other days. The reason for this was because the people who came provided the money that kept the house of prayer going. She went on to ask me not to pray that the statue wept on a Monday because on a Monday she went to Bingo.

I will not tell you what happened next but when I have reflected on the weekend I have found myself becoming quite a little depressed. I have wondered what we have done to people, to make them think, that the life of faith has anything to do with statues that move and weep. I have found myself overly concerned that people have got so caught up with the myriad of strange devotions that seem to surround us these days. I began to ask myself, what we have done to people, to make them believe that our life with God is dependent on how good we are or how many prayers we say.

It seems to me, that our life with God has got little to do with us and everything to do with a God who is pouring out love constantly. It is not about what we do for God but what God wants to do for us and all God wants to do is love us. The heart of God is love, the justice of God is mercy, the wrath of God is passionate, insane love for God's creatures.

All that God wants is for us to experience that love. That is what changes our hearts. That is what changes the way we see life. That is what brings faith alive. That is what makes us want to go to Church and to read the Bible and lets us know the truth that Jesus is risen from the dead. To somehow experience deeply within us the love that is freely given, freely poured out, and wants nothing in return, is to experience the heart of God more than anything else.

It does not depend on you. Please hear that! You cannot earn it or merit it. There is something in us that reacts to a free gift. We want to earn our salvation. The notion of God's love being freely given seems to go against every instinct of humanity. I am told that every religious path you can think of seems to be about earning love: the Buddhist eight fold path, the Hindu karma, the Jewish covenant, the Muslim code of law. All are about earning approval.

Only Christianity makes God's love unconditional and yet even we, with our awareness of love, try to reduce love to what we do. God will love us when we are good. God will love us if we act in a particular way. Yet God is love. The very nature of God is to love unconditionally. God's passion is God's children - you and me. God is passionate about us. God's concern is for us. God desires that intimacy with us that our hearts desire.

You cannot reduce God's love to being dependent on us, thinking it has got anything to do with our petty, puny attempts at being good and religious. It is God's gift. You are not going to get more of God's love because of what you do or less of it because of what you do not do. God is love and simply wants to love. Throughout the Church's long history there have been many great saints, mystics, and teachers who have known that truth. Read what some of them have said.

Pope Benedict XVI in his first encyclical said, 'the one God in whom Israel believes, loves with a personal love which is freely poured out'.

Most of the saints are remembered for their good works, the amount of love and compassion in their lives. St. Jerome is more often than not remembered for his bad temper! Despite that, his love for God was extraordinarily intense; He was above all a Scripture scholar, translating most of the First Testament from the Hebrew. When talking of God, Jerome said, 'love is not to be purchased'.

John Scottus lived from about 800 or 810 to around about 877 and is a major figure in the development of mystical spirituality in western European Christianity. He believed that God is both within humanity and beyond us and he said, 'God is properly called love because he is the cause of all love'.

Catherine of Siena is a saint, a mystic, and a doctor of the Church, as well as a patroness of Italy and of Europe. She was born in 1347, into a very large family, and she died in Rome in 1380. She entered the Third Order of the Dominicans at the age of sixteen. Catherine was sought out as a spiritual director and during one of her encounters with Christ, heard him say to her, 'I can love you more than you can love yourself and I watch over you a thousand times more carefully than you can watch over yourself'.

Julian of Norwich who lived between 1342 and 1416 is

internationally famous for her *Revelations of Divine Love*. She remains one of the most creative theologians, spiritual writers and mystics in the Christian tradition. In my opinion, if anyone should be canonised Julian should be. She said this of God, 'in his love he clothes us, enfolds and embraces us, that tender love completely surrounds us never to leave us.'

John of Ruysbroeck was a Flemish mystical writer who was a huge influence on mystical teaching in the late Middle Ages. He was born near Brussels in 1293, studied for the priesthood and was ordained in 1317. He eventually withdrew to a hermitage, near Soignes, and adopted the rule of the canons of St. Victor. He was beatified by Pope Pius X in 1908. When reflecting on God, John once wrote of God, 'the heat of his touch and love is so great that it would burn us up'.

Nicholas of Cusa was ordained a priest in about 1440, made a cardinal in Brixen, Italy, by Pope Nicholas V and in 1450 became bishop there. He was a learned man, skilled in theology, mathematics, philosophy, science, and the arts. In writing of God he said, 'you my God are love who loves'.

Therese of Lisieux, the much loved 19th century Carmelite entered the Carmel at the age of 15. She wanted to give her whole life to God. She was known to have great intimacy with God. Her very short life was plagued with sickness but she remained faithful to God and was rooted in love. After a long struggle with tuberculosis, she died on September 30, 1897, at the age of 24. She once wrote, 'however far you go in the spiritual life the simpler it all becomes, because it is all about love'.

Donald Coggan was the one hundred and first Archbishop of Canterbury from 1974 to 1980. Coggan was noted for his progressive views, supporting the ordination of women and fostering relations between Christians and Jews. He said, 'God loves us in our sin and through our sin and goes on loving us'.

Benedict XVI wrote, 'Christian faith lives on the discovery that not only is there such a thing as objective meaning, but this meaning knows me and loves me.'

Love is at the core of Christianity and to be a Disciple is, first and foremost, to know in the depths of your being that you are loved. That is what gives you security and encourages you to take the risks that the Scriptures tell us Disciples are to take.

There are all sorts of questions that arise when thinking about God's love and the primary one that most people ask me is, 'Does that mean I can do what I want and

God will always love me?' It is a non-question because when you have been overpowered by love, when you know the truth of grace, you only want to do what God wants. It is a love relationship. You will make mistakes but the focus of your life will be about love responding to love.

The second question I have been asked is what about all the awful things that happen in the world, what about poverty and heartache and natural disasters? What about wars and oppression? I do not know that I have any answers to those questions. I think that some of what happens could be put down to our own greed and selfishness and some things just do not have answers.

Once we know that we are loved by God it means, I think, that we see the world through different eyes. I know that because of the love that has been poured into my heart I see the world through different eyes. I am beginning to recognise the love of God all around me when I really look. God is there in the beauty of the world, in the smile of a child in the tears of brokenness. God is everywhere. It is that love that makes me see I am united to every human person and am called to work for unity so that others can see the love that holds us in being.

When I was working with people who lived on the streets I met a man called Peter who worked tirelessly for the poor and the impoverished. He spent hours each day trying to find accommodation, visiting hospitals and medical centres trying to get treatment for people. He could often be found sitting at the war memorial with the alcoholics. He paid out of his own money to buy food and cigarettes that he gave away freely. One day I asked him why he did all that he did. He began to tell me a story and as he did his eyes filled up. Many years earlier he had been working for a multi-national oil company. He lived the lifestyle of a top executive, flying all over the world, eating in the most expensive restaurants, staying in the most exclusive hotels. He worked hard; very hard, he told me, with a wry smile on his face, and he played hard too.

One day he was sent to Dar Es Salaam for a meeting with several other executives After the meeting and dinner he went to a club and as he was leaving in the early hours of the morning he was almost fell over a woman who was lying in the street. She reached out her hand and touched him begging for money. He shook her off and as he walked away he heard her call after him, 'help me, I too am a child of God'.

He got back to his hotel a little bit disturbed by the incident but it went out of his mind until he was packing a couple of days later. He was rooting in a drawer and a Gideon Bible fell open. He glanced at the page and saw the story of Dives and Lazarus. As he read, he said, the scales fell from his eyes and he realised that he was just like the rich man in the Gospel. Like Dives in the Gospel story, he was not particularly a bad man, but he knew he was not a good man either. He was just so concerned with himself that he did not even see the poverty around him. When he was faced with it as he had been in the encounter with the woman in the street, he simply walked away. The world was there to serve him and to make sure he had a good life. He had the power and those who were powerless were not even noticed.

He remembered the woman's words, 'I too am a child of God' and, he said, he wept. There and then, he vowed to do whatever he could to help as many human beings know the truth that they were beloved children of God. He told me that he was prepared to love whatever the cost to himself. That was why he did what he did.

If we have become aware of the truth of love in our lives, if we have begun to discover that there is nothing that can separate us from the love of God, then the invitation is to allow love to flow though us. Love invites us to love because every human person is a child of God. That is our common bond.

Each of the evangelists has his own particular thrust when writing his Gospel. Luke's Gospel was written for those who find themselves on the outside. He has a bias for the poor and the little ones, for those for whom society has little value. Lepers, Samaritans, women, tax collectors; you will find them all playing a part in Luke's Gospel.

Today it would be people who live on the edges, the kids who roam our estates, the old people who live terrified, those who find themselves alienated because of colour, creed, mental health issues, sexuality, or unacceptable behaviour.

Luke turns the social order upside down and always has Jesus sitting down with those who are on the edges. It is the most scandalising piece of writing because it says that all are of value and all are welcome. No-one is left out in Luke's Gospel. Luke challenges us to love the unlovable. Diarmuid O'Murchu in his book, *Inclusivity - a Gospel Mandate* says, 'Christianity stands or falls on its fidelity to the outsider'.

I am not saying that this is easy. For years I worked with people who lived on the streets and it is not easy to love those who frighten you and swear at you and spit at you. It is not easy to sit with a smelly man of the road who is crying because of his drunkenness and the hopelessness he feels.

It is never easy to be the forgiver when all you experience is rejection and antagonism. It is hard to be the one who stands up against the tide and speaks in the name of love. If you love you will be persecuted.

Love is not easy. It is the narrow road that the Gospels speak of and yet it is the only reality that changes hearts and minds and makes life worth living and when you have tasted love and shared love you will give your life for love.

The invitation is to look at those attitudes within that would stop us loving. What is it within me that makes me exclusive rather than inclusive? What is it within me that makes me walk past those in need? What is it in me that makes me self-righteous and arrogant? What is it within me that reacts to the asylum seeker and the refugee, to the street people? What is it within me that does not allow the love that has freed me and liberated me to flow into the lives of those who are broken and hurting?

The love that is in the heart of God can change anything and everything. All it takes is that we allow that love to flow through us and that we be faithful to the truth of love.

I always find it interesting that when people are asked

about their experience of faith coming alive, almost to a person they will talk of their desire to be united. Firstly with God, then with others, the world, and, the more insightful, with themselves. Unity is the work of God and those who enter into relationship with Jesus and who begin to discover what life is about will want unity. It seems to be that the desire for unity is one of the ways in which God blesses us. There are some writers who say that without that desire for unity there has been no genuine experience of God. It's a fundamental response to the reality of God.

John Donne wrote the famous line, 'No man is an island' or in today's politically correct terms, 'No one is an island'. We are in relationship with one another whether we like it or not. We are connected with those who have gone before us and those who will come after us and those who share this planet with us. Those who allow the reign of God's love to begin to happen within them, recognise the call to enter into deep intimate vulnerable relationships with other people. That is why Jesus invites us not to judge or condemn one another but rather to treat one another with real reverence and respect.

The same is true for the created order. Be passionate for God's creation. It seems to me that we have to enter into the issues that are threatening to destroy the incredible gift of the world. A person who wants real unity will be concerned about global warming and the destruction of rain forests, and the way in which we plunder natural resources for our own selfish needs. It is right to be concerned about the nuclear issue and the need to live simply so that others can simply live. We are to live in this world showing others the truth of humanity and the beauty of the world and sharing with others the invitation to live our lives for the sake of unity.

As we enter into relationship with ourselves, others, and the world, we will begin to sense the call of the divine to enter into real intimacy and connectedness. We will begin to get in touch with the God who is in all things. Incarnation is about the coming together of the divine and the human. It is all about integration and unity flowing from the source that is God.

THREE

THE FLOW OF
PERFECT RELATIONSHIP

I once went on retreat to a house in the Lake district run by an order of semi-enclosed sisters. I had been struggling inside myself and I wanted to be silent for a while. I have always found that in silence I have experienced over time a sense of unconditional love. In the past that sense of love had that really liberated me and brought deep inner healing so I had come to the Lakes looking for that.

I wanted the silence to help me live in a way that becomes a dance of love with God. I wanted the silence to open my eyes and heart again so that I could see the presence of God everywhere. I was beginning to let myself become clouded and jaded. I was unable to see God all around me. I think I had stopped looking and my sense of gratitude at the gift of this world and of life itself was beginning to dissipate.

I have known the truth, that when we enter into that dance of love, we live in what we call the kingdom of God and that is what brings us life. I know that anything else is less than God has in mind for us and stops us living life to the full and what happens is that we die within. Silence restores us and brings us well-springs of hope within that we never knew existed. It is the source of our power to bring unconditional love into the world we live in.

So for me it was wonderful to be in the silence and more wonderful to be surrounded by the beautiful land-scape of the lake district in all its magnificence. Just driving up to the retreat house I felt my spirit begin to lift and hope again. When I arrived I was shown to my room which had great views from the windows. Even those views seemed to calm me deeply within and to begin to pour balm on my jangled nerve endings. I lay on the bed and fell into a deep sleep. I was awoken by the bell calling the house to supper. When I arrived the sister who met me had asked if I minded having my meals with the community who ate in silence. I was their only guest that week and it would save them setting up another dining room. I said that would be fine.

I made my way to the community dining room and having been shown my seat settled down. I took some food and then, as an inveterate people watcher, began to look around me. There were about twelve sisters in the room. Some of them were very elderly and some younger. Nobody spoke, as was their custom, but they smiled and acknowledged one another. Those who were more able helped those who were less able to get their food and settle into their seats.

Then the music began to play. If you have ever seen the film Shawshank Redemption, you cannot fail to remember the scene, when one prisoner breaks into the governor's office. He locks himself in and puts a record to play over the tannoy system. The voice of an Italian opera singer fills the air. It is the most amazing moment in the film when the prisoners, hearing this music, stop working and talking and look around them as this beauty breaks into their drab prison lives.

I have always seen it as an experience of the reality of God where beauty transforms and heals pain and ugliness. It has always moved me. As the music began to play in that dining room in the Lake district I was taken beyond myself and felt as though I was encountering something which was much deeper and more wonderful than anything I had experienced before. In the silence God was touching me but on reflection I have realised something else. It was also in that silent community of women that God was touching me, and throughout the time I spent with them, restoring me.

It was the quiet dignity with which they treated one another. It was the smiles they had for one another and the way that they looked after one another's needs that spoke to my heart of the reality of God in our midst. My time with them was an experience of God's presence.

Theologians and philosophers will tell us the truth that God is beyond imagination and beyond language. Even words like all powerful, omnipotent, invincible supreme fall short of describing the reality of God. Nothing can capture that reality. Human cognitive powers at best get a glimpse of who God is, which of course means that not even theology or church dogma can capture or explain God as much as they try. There is always more to discover which is why faith is such an exciting journey.

So God can never be completely understood, known or captured by the human mind. However, generations of believers from our Jewish roots onwards have recognised, experienced, even tasted the reality of God in their ordinary lives. The Scriptures are full of stories of people who experience deep intimacy with God, think of the stories of Moses and David or Peter and Paul and countless others. Ronald Rolheiser says that 'God is Someone and Something that we live within and which can flow through our veins.'

In the first chapter of this book we reflected on God as perfect unity and how that unity is the blue print for all of creation. I think because of that truth we always live in God whether we acknowledge it or not. We live in God when we love, forgive and have compassion on others. I think John in his first letter recognised that when he wrote 'if we love one another, God lives in us and his love is made complete in us.' The heart of all truth is that God is love. Love isn't something God has created, but the very essence of who God is. God can only love. Anyone who shows God's self giving love is reflecting God for the world. That means that God operates outside the parameters that we so often put on God. God is being made present wherever there is love. Such love is 'made complete' when it comes from God through us and brings life to others.

More than that we live in God, in moments of brokenness and pain too. Christ is living and dying and rising all around us every day in our lives and in the lives of others. We are caught up in something that is eternal. The Christ we have been given is far more than we can ever imagine. How do we live with the paradox of death and resurrection? I guess all we can do is ponder the mystery and let it bear fruit within us. I think that fruit is the awareness that the Paschal mystery is in the very stuff of our lives. Even when it appears that we are in the throes of a crisis, the seeds of resurrection are at work. I guess the challenge is to know that it is in the DNA of creation. It is to know that the moments of death we all experience have within them the seeds of resurrection. It is also to know that in order for resurrection to happen, death has to be at the core of it. That is the Paschal mystery and the universal pattern that all of creation follows. Christ makes sense of what happens to us all without exception.

When I was a student, learning theology, we used to talk of the processions in God and the truth that within the Godhead is a flow of relationship, creator God, saviour God and enlivening God. Father, Son and Spirit all flowing into and out from each other. If that perfect relationship is the model for creation then every flow of relationship that we live in is an experience of God. God is present and can be experienced in community, in family and in Parish. God can be experienced wherever there is friendship and love, forgiveness and reconciliation.

Henri Nouwen once said 'When I trust deeply that today God is truly with me and holds me safe in a divine embrace, guiding every one of my steps I can let go of my anxious need to know how tomorrow will look, or what will happen next month or next year. I can be fully where I am and pay attention to the many signs of God's love within me and around me.'

I love that phrase 'Many signs of God's love within me

and around me'. It intimates that God can be experienced in the ordinariness of life. St Bonaventure used to talk of the footprints of God being everywhere. The truth is that we find God at the kitchen sink or at the dinner table as much as in our churches or in our theology books. We find God when people love one another and forgive one another much more than in the practice of right dogma or even in knowing the correct doctrine. That's what I discovered in that experience in the Lake district. God was in the very stuff of humanity. The human reflects the divine, if imperfectly, and there is no surer place to find God than in the simple flow of human relationships and in the beauty of creation.

That means of course that the distinction between something being holy and something being secular is a false understanding. Richard Rohr in his book *Eager to Love: The Alternative Way of Francis of Assisi* says 'There are not sacred and profane things, places, and moments. There are only sacred and desecrated things, places, and moments and it is we who desecrate them by our blindness and lack of reverence. It is one sacred unverse, and we are all a part of it.' There is nothing inside of which God cannot be found. Everything is created in the image and likeness of God and the whole of the universe reflects that truth.

Ronald Rolheiser says, 'The most pernicious heresies that block us from properly knowing God are not those of formal dogma, but those of a culture of individualism that invite us to believe that we are self-sufficient, that we can have community and family on our own terms, and that we can have God without dealing with each other.'

I think what he is inviting us into is a process of conversion. In order to experience the reality of God a great inner change of movement is invited of us. That is because I think we understand the truth of community less than any other people who have gone before us. We are born in what is probably the most individualistic culture the world has ever produced. We live in the age of the individual and we have forgotten our need of each other. Everything is about me and my fulfilment. When that is our base line from which we operate then we have a hard time in really accepting that we are called into relationship. Of course when we forget that truth, it is impossible to live within the flow of God and unity and harmony are almost an impossibility.

So a great conversion is asked of us in order that we live in the flow of relationship. All the great spiritual gurus of our time recognise the need to focus our attention away from ourselves. This enables us to see that we are part of something bigger.

Winnie was a retired nurse that my mum was friendly with. They were both part of the Ladies of Charity in the Parish where I grew up. They went to Lourdes and Walsingham together and day pilgrimages to places like Fernehough in Preston or Bala in Wales. She was a much loved member of the Parish community and I can still picture her in her tweed skirts and her pretty blouses and, of course, her sensible lace up brogues! Winnie was a very genteel lady who always spoke as if she was apologising for something. She lived in a small council flat in a block designed for senior citizens. In her flat were remnants of furniture from her parents home which were polished regularly. She was always full of stories of her nephews and nieces of whom she was very proud. Whenever we called to see Winnie, tea was always served in small, delicate china cups and cake on plates that matched with cake forks and napkins.

The one exception to Winnie's gentility was her driving. She had a red mini which she drove like a whirling dervish. She travelled at breakneck speeds, took corners on two wheels and paid little heed to traffic regulations. We were always terrified of being driven anywhere by Winnie and would go to any lengths to avoid it. That mini, however, was her pride and joy not because it was a material possession but because it enabled Winnie to serve.

That little red car was used day in and day out to help others. Anyone who need a lift anywhere could guarantee that Winnie would stop what she was doing and help. They might look a little green when they arrived at their destination but arrive they did for whatever their appointment was.

She once told me that before she retired she wondered how she would keep a car on the road. Pensions were not particularly generous in the 1960's but a member of her family had bought it for her or given the money for it on the proviso that she used it to help others. As she told me the story she had a smile on her face when she said 'after all life is not just about me. It is more about others and their needs'.

Megan McKenna in her book *'And Morning Came: Scriptures of the Resurrection'* writes 'Conversion, constant conversion, is the message of the Gospel.' We have to move from the 'I' to the 'we'. Most people are not really willing to make that conversion and so Church becomes something that we do rather than something that we are. We do not recognise that we are called to live in the flow of perfect relationship caring for one another, loving one another, accepting one another. It was a real shock to me to discover that I am not the sum total of the universe. There is more to life than me! My life belongs to God and to others.

This lack of recognition has consequences. We can allow the scandal of starvation to take place because it happens in Africa. We can allow the scandal of war to take place because it is justified. We can gossip about people's misfortunes. We can allow the pain of division to exist within our Christian communities. We can hold on to unforgiveness and bitterness and anger. Sadly, all the time that we live in these ways we are not reflecting the true nature of God nor of creation. We are by our very nature called to unity. Ronald Rolheiser said in one of his weekly reflections, 'There is no level of reality where one does not see the relentless deep pull inside of all things towards a unity, community, fusion, and oneness beyond self.'

In order to realise this unity, prayer and reflection are of vital importance. Where do I allow my own individualism, where the only things that matter are 'me and my needs', to, if not die, at least take second place. Where am I allowing myself to be challenged to live for the good of all? Where am I being encouraged to use my resources for the sake of others? How am I responding to the invitation to live a life of unity, in the flow of perfect relationship? I guess we have to be willing to face those inner realities that make us selfish and unwilling to serve. We can look at the attitudes of mind that we have towards those who are other than we are. Dare we reach out to migrant workers, refugees and asylum seekers? Have we the courage to stand against the tide of hatred and discrimination that seems to be sweeping across our country and laying waste to the dignity of so many?

We can be inclusive rather than exclusive and by our silence challenge those who would be sexist racist or homophobic. It is the small things that we do that move the mountains. Jesus told us that the poor would be with us always. I think we know that in our society that is not always the materially poor. I think it was St Teresa of Calcutta who recognised that the spiritual poverty of the west is as bad if not worse than material poverty. So we can open our eyes to those in need who live in our street. We can learn to smile and acknowledge those that everybody else walks past or treats with suspicion. We can draw others into the flow of love through our concern and care for them. All of that is living in the flow of perfect relationship. It is revealing the image of God to the world but it calls for deep radical conversion.

Archbishop Helder Camara who for many years was the Archbishop of Recife in Brazil understood this. He had a very deep sense that the very poorest people were his family. If he heard that the police had arrested someone who had no voice he would ring them and say 'I believe that you have arrested my brother' and the police would apologise and say 'please come and collect him'. When Dom Helder arrived at the station he would be told 'this man does not have the same family name as you. How can he be your brother?' Dom Helder would always answer 'All people are my brothers and sisters.'

A few years ago I read a book by Timothy Radcliffe, the Dominican Priest, which was a reflection on the seven words or phrases that were spoken from the Cross and I used them for Lenten reflection. One of the points he made in the book was when he was reflecting on the words 'woman this is your son, son this is your mother'. He said that 'the community born at the foot of the cross propels us beyond the boundaries of our blood relations. We are invited to recognise that every person is our brother and sister and mother and father.'

When I worked in Vauxhall which is a part of inner city Liverpool I met many wonderful people who struggled with life and yet were always willing to share what they had. One day I was asked to take communion to a very old man and his equally elderly wife. They lived in a small flat with their middle aged daughter.

Their home was clean and bright. The daughter obviously loved her mum and dad. She worked and when she was working during the day, her elder sister came and sat with the parents and made their lunch and did whatever was needed. The old man was called Tom and he, and Kathleen his wife, were a fund of stories about old Liverpool. They would tell me of rag and bone men and the markets of Scotland Road. He had been a docker and she had cleaned offices to make ends meet. They had seven children, the two I had met and five others who lived away but who came as often as they could. One of the stories that he was fond of telling was of the night they had been bombed out during the Blitz.

Tom had flat feet and so was unable to join the forces but he became a fire warden. He would often describe the night that he went out during the blitz and after long hard fire fighting came home to find that the street he lived in had been raised to the ground. Thankfully Kathleen and the children were safe, he said, and they soon found somewhere else to live but many neighbours had been killed including Tom's brother and sister who lived next door.

The visits went on for some months until eventually Tom died. I went to see Kathleen and Joan, their daughter, to arrange the funeral. Joan made some tea and then began to talk and at one point I said to her 'Did your dad have any favourite hymns?' She looked a bit puzzled and then said 'O Tom wasn't my Dad.' She then went on to explain that she and her sister lived with their parents just up the street from Tom, Kathleen and their family. In the bombing their mum and dad had been killed and Tom and Kathleen had taken them in. She went on to tell me that it was never a formal adoption. 'I guess after the war nobody really thought about those things' she smiled. Joan then went on to tell me that at no point had Tom or Kathleen ever made any distinction between their own children or she and her sister. Neither had their children. 'We are family' she said smiling at Kathleen who smiled back and reached out to hold her hand. I left that house in tears that day because I had been shown a lived out Gospel truth. That we as human beings are family to one another. We have a common bond which is accentuated in Christ.

So the challenge is to open our eyes and see that we are to live in the flow of perfect relationship. That means, of course, that we have then to do everything in our power to work for peace and reconciliation all around us and all over the world. It is then that flow of relationship that is God and which we are caught up in can become a reality. Pope Francis recently quoted Paul VI in his homily for the closing of the Second Vatican Council, 8 December 1965 when he said this 'Let us remember Paul VI's words: 'For the Catholic Church, no one is a stranger, no one is excluded, no one is far away'. Indeed, we are a single human family that is

journeying on toward unity, making the most of
solidarity and dialogue among peoples in the multi-
plicity of differences.

As we begin to recognise our call to find God in the
midst of relationship unity and harmony, then it
becomes clear that everything that works against unity
and fusion has to be healed and transformed. You know
all God wants is that humanity be submerged in the
vastness of love. Pierre Teilhard de Chardin the French
idealist philosopher and Jesuit priest whose philosophy
drew together science, philosophy, mysticism, and
poetry brilliantly. He wrote 'Love is the affinity which
links and draws together the elements of the world...
Love, in fact, is the agent of universal synthesis.' It is
love that is freely given because it is the essence of God
and the blue print for the whole of the created order. It
is not something we have to earn. It is not something
we deserve. It is simply there, poured out everywhere
and in everything and all we have to do is trust it and
believe it.

When we mirror that truth by the pouring out of our
lives we enable others to stand in the immensity of love
that knows no end. We enable others to be caught
up in the love that underpins everything. That we so
often do not manage to do that is why we need deep
conversion day in and day out.

When we really do begin to enter into the process of conversion and transformation then we begin to recognise the presence of God all around us. We see the nature of God in the very stuff of the universe. We are caught up in the flow of perfect relationship and all we want is to have harmony and union with everyone and everything. We cannot see or enter into what underpins the universe without the grace of God and unless the spirit opens our eyes and helps us to see.

FOUR

DESIRING GOD

A few years ago I received a phone call to ask if I was available to speak at a local gathering. It was a series of meetings to help people explore the Scriptures. I was to be the first speaker if I was available and the topic was to be 'What is the Bible for'. I try never to say no to invitations unless I am diametrically opposed to the stance the organisers take; so I agreed, thinking this would be a good opportunity, to share with a mainly Catholic audience my love of the Scriptures.

I did quite a lot of work for the session and was as pleased as I ever am with the result. Armed with my computer I set off. When I arrived I was really disappointed there were only about ten people there. Most of them were elderly and probably went to everything in the Parish regardless of what it was. I know those people need feeding as much as anyone else, but I was hoping for a more eclectic mix, so that we could get a conversation going. I was a bit disgruntled but went ahead with setting things up. I did not know how I was to be challenged that night.

As we started, the young man who had phoned me introduced me. John had obviously done his research and found out quite a lot about me but as part of his introduction he shared something of his faith journey. He said that he had fallen in love with God many years ago and that the Scriptures had come alive for him and he wanted others to have the same experience. John spoke very hesitatingly and was obviously unused to public speaking. I doubt that he had ever challenged anybody in any way. Indeed when I told him afterwards how challenged I felt, he apologised and I had to reassure him that it was fine.

The unwitting challenge was this: John said that since his initial encounter with God, his desire for God increased every day. He described how he woke up each day thirsting for God with such depth that at times it took his breath away and reduced him to tears. As he spoke I found myself asking the question, 'Do I still desire God that much?' I knew at the time that I once had desired God that much, but had the routine of a Christian life in ministry blunted the desire for God?

I think it is a huge challenge to those of us who are religious people because we are the very ones who are supposed to be open to God and in fact we are often the very ones who are not. I often think, you know, we keep God locked up and safe. We keep God in the arena of piety and devotion. God who is supremely free, filled with the wildness of the spirit; we try to tame and domesticate that God.

Is the God we say we desire a God that we have created for ourselves? Are we comfortable with the image of God that we have or is our understanding of God changing daily. Do we open ourselves to the unexpected encounter and the wildness of a God who cannot be contained within the walls of a Church, the pages of a book, or the images we have in our minds? I guess if we can keep God safe and respectable, all the better for us because it means we do not have to change and let this God into our lives. I think the truth is that God is always more than we can imagine.

If, as I believe, God is perfect unity, then the blue-print for the universe is unity. All of creation beats together in one united pulse of colour, movement, and breath. Human beings are at their happiest when they are united with one another and with creation. To desire God is to desire unity with every living reality. I recently read that some ancient peoples thought that the human soul was a piece of 'divine fire' that had somehow become separated from God. They believed that this divine fire blazed within us. They also thought that this divine fire was always trying to return to God, searching to be reunited with every living thing wanting

God above all. It was that search to be intimately united that makes most human beings restless within. For the ancient people, we were on fire because our immortal soul was trying to escape from a mortal body.

I think that fire, that relentless pressure, is not only in the soul, it is in everything else as well. Ronald Rolheiser says that 'the cosmos is all of a piece. The chemicals in your hand and in your brain were forged by the same furnace, the furnace of the stars.' He says 'the story of life, body and soul, is written in DNA and relentless yearning lies just as much in the cosmos and the DNA as it lies in our hearts and souls.'

The longing and yearning that is within all of us drives us and empowers us to look for more. What has been defined as divine fire is the Spirit of God, groaning and praying through us. I think this endless quest for unity with God and with the created order is what the letter to the Romans is talking about when it tells us that when 'we do not know how to pray, the Spirit of God prays through us, in groans too deep for words'. At its root, all longing is for the things of God. All life, all energy, whether conscious or unconscious, yearns for love, joy, peace, patience, goodness, and unity.

Only God can fill that yearning and desire. Search for that encounter with the living God where God delights to meet us face to face. It can be in pain and suffering. It can be in the midst of joy. It will be in answered prayer and unanswered prayer. One thing I am sure of is that it will be in life and not in a false world of spirituality which is rooted nowhere and in nothing.

I am sure that anyone reading this will know that the litmus test for this searching and desire for unitive living has nothing to do with being in Church and doing pious things. It has everything to do with how, and to what extent, we are prepared to love our neighbour; the poor, the ignored, the uncomfortable to be with.

I remember once working, as a student, in a local hospice. It was difficult work, washing patients and helping them with their toileting, as well as the emotional strain when they died. I came home most evenings emotionally wrung out.

One of the patients there was called Jim. He was in the latter stages of motor neurone disease and was bed-ridden. His disease was such that he could no longer speak and he had to be fed through a tube in his stomach. He had lost huge amounts of weight and from stays in hospital had developed very painful smelly bedsores. His eyes were very sensitive to light and so he was always in a darkened room. No family ever visited him. Despite his inability to speak, his bitterness and anger flowed from him and made him a very difficult person to be with.

His one visitor was a man whom, I was told by other staff, was a Buddhist monk who came at least twice a week. This man would simply sit next to Jim's bed holding his hand. This man's visits which lasted at least an hour seemed to be the one thing that filled Jim with peace. One day I met the monk coming out of Jim's room and something made me ask the very crass question, 'Why do you come to see Jim every few days?' The monk looked at me and smiled and said, 'I come because here I find God'. He then smiled and left me to ruminate about what he had said.

I have thought about that experience on many occasions over the years. I have come to the conclusion that most of us have a very long way to travel in order to get to the place where we find God in the least of these. Faith propels us beyond human expectation that we do the right thing. Faith in the goodness of God demands much more. The more is the deep inner change that propels us into dialogue with the world and our brothers and sisters where we meet the God for whom we long. If you never had a prayer answered, never saw someone's life changed, never experienced healing, would you still want God? Are you hungry for God and for more and more of God, because if you are hungry for God you will find God, who is always present.

There are at least two ways in the Christian tradition of understanding what God is doing. There is a sense in which they both co-exist. One is the incarnational tradition and the other the redemptive tradition. Throughout history there has always been an emphasis on one or the other.

Incarnational understanding emphasises the presence of God within humanity and it appreciates values like growth and process. In the Scriptures the images that are incarnational are the leaven and the mustard seed. People who grew up with a healthy worldview and understanding of humanity tend to see life through the incarnational because that has been their life's experience of gradual growth. Its strength can be found in the way in which we understand humanity and our own growth as people. The weakness is that we can take God for granted, and become humanists where growing into the person we are supposed to be and being nice is enough. That can lead to a very shallow understanding of incarnational theology and it certainly is a temptation.

The Redemptive tradition is all about intervention and breakthrough. It loves the spectacular. Easter is the redemptive Christ who is forever breaking into history. It is the other part of the mystery of Christ. Redemptive understanding always looks for God to break in. It does not presume that it can understand God's pattern. It allows God to be the God of surprises. It allows God to be God. That is its strength. Its weakness is that it does not appreciate the ordinary. It can miss the God of the present moment with its preoccupation with the spectacular. The word Parousia is best described as the coming, the forever coming, of God. The Parousia is the eternal entry of God into history. It never ends and it is happening now for those who are able to see.

I guess the place of peace is the creative tension in the middle, the place that says God is both redemptive and incarnational. If within us there is a hunger and desire for God that consumes us, if we are searching and looking and wanting, then however God comes, and God is always coming, our eyes will be open and we will recognise God. It is then that everything becomes sacred and holy and we begin to see the unity that lies behind everything and which draws us more deeply into unity with everything. It is then we discover God and through the divine fire within, the human soul is at peace.

I think the primary revelation of the Spirit in these years has been that we are loved by God. I came across this quotation recently from Pedro Arrupe who was

Jesuit Father General from 1965 to 1983. 'Nothing is more practical than finding God, that is, than falling in love in an absolute, final way. What you are in love with, what seizes your imagination, will affect everything. It will decide what will get you out of bed in the mornings, what you will do with your evenings, how you spend your week-ends, what you read, who you know, what breaks your heart, and what amazes you with love and gratitude. Fall in love, stay in love, and it will decide everything.'

The transforming power of God happens within us when we fall into the mystery of God. It occurs when we stop trying to understand and simply fall into grace which is that place where we know that we are held and embraced by mystery and otherness. Those two words have been occupying my attention for the last couple of months. Mystery and otherness point us back through the pages of the First Testament to the dark, wild, otherness of a God who will not be trapped, confined, caged, or domesticated; a God that the prophets understood, a God who could be found in the most extraordinary of places. Those two words invite us to seek God everywhere and in everything which inevitably leads us to see the unity that underpins everything.

I recently was very privileged to meet a woman, who in

the eyes of the world, had nothing. Betty has Downs Syndrome and because of it has severe learning difficulties. I met her in a day centre where a friend of mine works. As I walked in Betty flew across the room and threw her arms around me. She looked up at me and with the innocence, simplicity, and beauty that lies at the heart of many people like her, she smiled and said, 'I love you'.

When I was telling my friend what had happened after afterwards she said to me that working in the day centre had transformed her understanding of life. People like Betty in their simplicity and honesty simply saw goodness and love at the centre of everything. This had made her challenge her way of viewing the world and the people who lived in it. She told me that her cynicism and hardness had been softened and that she was now more aware of God than she had ever been before. Sometimes we are given extraordinary gifts.

The prophets, and Isaiah primarily, point us beyond our Religious existence to a way of life that is rooted in intimacy with a God who wants to overwhelm us with the power of love. Several of the prophets, particularly Isaiah, Amos, and Ezekiel, condemn much of our religious practice because it can stop us entering the mystery. It can make us closed, narrow, partisan, and self righteous. When that happens we become virtually unable to encounter God. Our souls can never be at one with God and with the whole of creation because we are not looking for God everywhere in creation and in every brother and sister of faith or no faith.

That is why I find it so sad that most people seem to prefer unthreatening religion to the living God. Most people do not seem to want the God who breaks into our lives, quietly or spectacularly, who shatters our understandings and who turns us upside down. Most people do not want the sort of life that discovers God's presence everywhere and in everything, even in that which is other. It is too threatening and challenging. It is far easier to go to Church and live by a particular moral code than to let the divine fire within seek God in the most extraordinary of places. It is often easier for us to keep God small and manageable. This is how God acts! This what God wants! We have been so guilty of thinking we know how God works and where God will be found. How do we know? All we can really do is let life and God happen. Then we will be led into that place of deep connection with everything.

Just recently I was speaking at a conference about the word of God and how the word can enable us to fall into grace. That is just another way of saying falling into the mystery of God where everything is about the unity and harmony of creation. I spoke of getting in touch with the deep desire of my heart, which I know is for God and the things of God. I went on to share that when you become aware of that desire, you move beyond the need to simply please God or live for God both of which are good but you begin to realise that there is more. It is the search for intimacy that brings deep inner peace. It is the encounter that tells us we are loved beyond our wildest dreams so that nothing else matters. It is the recognition of harmony within us and all around us.

When I came off the stage a woman followed me out and collapsed in my arms. She was weeping and was in a terrible state. I half pulled her and carried her into a room where she told me of her desire for God that she thought could never be fulfilled because of something she had done that she was unable to forgive herself for. Most of the time she managed to contain herself. However this day, listening to me talking about falling into grace, she was overwhelmed by her desire for God. The thought that her deep desire could never be fulfilled, as though it depended on her, caused her to despair deeply, hence her collapse into my arms.

We chatted for some time and we prayed and thank God she discovered that she could let go of the guilt, forgive herself and fall into grace, harmony, connectivity, and unity. That is what we are all invited to do and when we do it we begin to experience our longing for God being fulfilled and life becomes a dance of intimacy with a wild, freeing God who is everywhere. We then become more and more aware of the call to deep unity.

Johann Wolfgang von Goethe, was a German poet and playwright, considered the greatest German literary figure of the modern era. Goethe defines that longing for God that need for intimacy with God as 'a desire for higher love-making', a longing to embrace the world and make love to it, as God does. If we are searching for God and longing for God and desiring God then God will reveal Godself in the stuff of this world and in the harmony that exists between everything in the created order. Van Goethe goes on to say that 'such a desire, if correctly fostered, will wreak a painful but wonderful spiritual havoc within us; it will make us 'insane for the light', wild with the desire to transmute ourselves, grow wings like the butterfly, and fly off; not to escape the world, but to die to all the things that prevent us from, here and now, already making love to the whole world.'

Longing for God, desire for God, searching for God in the very stuff of this world, is always a transforming reality within us. It creates the energy within to change as we search more and more deeply. After all, whether we like it or not, change is at the core of the Gospel we say we follow. The heart of the message of Jesus is summed up in a little Greek word that we translate very safely as repent. Saying that you are sorry for your sins can be very self-satisfying. The word we translate as repent in Greek is metanoia; I seem to spend an awful lot of time talking and writing about metanoia but it is because it is at the heart of the Gospel.

The process of metanoia is all about what God wants to do within us not about what we want to do for God. It might be best translated as 'turn your mind around'. In terms of this book it could well be that we are being invited to move from our narrow separatist place where God is in some things but not in others to a place where we see God everywhere and begin to understand the unity of all creation. To enter into metanoia is to let the soul, the divine fire, the image and likeness of God, reign within us. As that happens we move into that place of cognitive unity and the very ground on which we base our lives begins to shift. Then we do indeed turn and face in a completely new direction.

So Gospel metanoia is all about our very beings transforming so that we begin to live with a different understanding of life and of the world. We begin to see and understand the oneness and harmony which underpins everything. It is far deeper than constantly saying sorry and it never depends on us but on God.

Then as that call to be united with everything and everyone shatters our narrowness and calls us beyond our limited imagination to be open to the ever-coming God, we begin to ask questions: Are my eyes open to the God who is all around me? Are my eyes open to the God of the present moment? Where am I looking for God? We do not have yesterday or tomorrow, just this moment, and it seems to me that the call of the Gospel is to be open to the gift of meeting the Lord, who is always present in the moment we have but we have to be longing and searching and looking for God.

That moment of meeting or encounter is the transforming moment, the one which revolutionises our inner being as we discover that deep truth that in the very fabric of the created order is the reality of God. It is then that we enter the reality of the Kingdom of God. The kingdom is not about the future, when we get to heaven, as so many of us seem to think it is. It is about the present moment and living that moment to the full, even the moments that are sad and painful. So the challenge is to open ourselves to the spirit of God all around us in everything. Then we will become immersed into the real, wild presence of the God of the prophets and enter into the discovery of the universal plan of unity.

I was reading somewhere recently about human

emptiness. The author said this: 'The proud intellectual penitentiary of atheistic secularism thinks it has sentenced God to solitary confinement, imprisoned divinity for life behind strong bars of reason and razor wire of patronising superiority, and thrown away the key. Yet the emptiness remains.'

Ignatius of Loyola used to talk about the God shaped hole that is within each one of us. Despite our technological advancements and our psychological advancements which have almost pushed humanity away from God, the yearning within our spirits for cognitive unity does not go away.

When you look at the miracles of Jesus, it is interesting to see that so many of them are connected to opening up or otherwise healing someone's eyes, ears, or tongue. These miracles always have more than a physical significance. The eyes of the blind are opened in order to see more deeply and spiritually; The ears of the deaf are opened in order to hear things more deeply; and tongues are set free so that we speak words that reconcile and draw humanity together.

What Jesus is doing in these miracles is attaching the eyes, ears, and tongue to the soul, that divine fire within, so that what a person is now seeing, hearing, and speaking is not bitterness, hurt, and pettiness, which always separate and divide, but rather those things that take us to that place of unity and deep harmony.

So get in touch with your desire for God. Let the spirit of God within you, that divine fire, open you up to discover God who is everywhere. Let your eyes, your ears, your mouths be opened as you are invited to move beyond yourself and be united with all creation and therefore with God who is in everything.

FIVE

UNITY IN CHRIST

I love the letter to the Colossians with its beautiful imagery and language and so in this chapter I would like to reflect a little on that letter. First, I would like to tell you Sarah's story. When I was first ordained I was sent to the town of St Helens where I was a full time youth chaplain. One of the schools I worked in was a high school for girls run by the Notre Dame sisters. It was there that I met Sarah. She was bright and attractive and was part of the chaplaincy group. Her GCSE results had been disappointing so Sarah was re-sitting her exams. One of the sisters who knew her well said that she had not fulfilled her potential. I was soon to find out why.

One afternoon I came across Sarah crying in the sixth form common room. Through her sobs she told me that her mum had been diagnosed with multiple sclerosis nine years earlier when Sarah was eight. Her dad was unable to cope with the situation and left. Sarah and her three younger siblings stayed with her mum. She told me that at first things had been fine. Her mum had few symptoms and managed things quite well. As the years went on the disease began to take hold, until now Sarah was in effect her mum's carer, and also looked after the younger children.

She told me that her mum was in a wheel-chair and was picked up most days to go to a day centre. Sarah coped with cooking, cleaning, looking after her mum's personal needs, and dealing with the other children. Was it any wonder that she had not managed to fulfil her potential? She was so upset that day because she had gone home at lunchtime to find that her mum had not been picked up to go to the day centre. When she reached for the phone to find out why, she had fallen out of the chair and had been lying on the floor for most of the morning. Sarah had picked her up, got one of the neighbours to come and sit with her for the afternoon and come back to school for her classes. She was in no fit state to try to study so I took her to the chapel and, because she was a person of faith, prayed with her for a while and then she helped me clear a cupboard out, just to take her mind off things.

The next day the school got in touch with the social services and after a while a package was put together to help Sarah's mum stay at home and have enough care so that Sarah did not feel quite as responsible. Eventually she had more time for herself. As she managed to come to some of the events that we put on around the town her relationship with God began to grow and blossom. She began to read and pray the Scriptures. She spent time in quiet each day and eventually passed her exams and went to study theology at a local university.

As the years have gone on that relationship with God has deepened. Sarah is now happily married, a teacher, with three children of her own and life is good. Central to that life is her deep intimate connection with a God who can be found in all things and who draws all things together. Her favourite book in the Scriptures is the letter to the Colossians because she says it has helped her to see the connections between everything in Christ. It is almost as though Sarah has fallen into the bigger picture.

For me that begs a question. Is the God we say we desire a God that we have created for ourselves, that we are comfortable with? Or is our understanding of God changing daily as we open ourselves to the unexpected encounter and the wildness of a God who, as I have always written, cannot be contained within the walls of a Church, the pages of a book, or the images we have in our minds? God is always more. The Christ we have been given is more than we can imagine.

Maybe to recognise this Christ who is of Cosmic proportions, we have to become mystics. In the early

1960s the Jesuit theologian Karl Rahner said that if Western Christianity did not rediscover its mystical foundations, we might as well close the doors of the churches because we will have lost the primary reason for our existence. I guess by mysticism he was talking about an inner experience of the reality of God, rather than just believing in dogma and doctrine. Believe it or not, all the great spiritual traditions in the world recognise that it is possible to experience God. An openness to an experience of God moves us from a small narrow understanding to an awareness of the Cosmic Christ in whom all things find their meaning.

One of the most beautiful aspects of the letter to the Colossians is its author's understanding of the intimate relationship between the cosmic Christ and the created order. The author of Colossians seems to think that Jesus, the Christ, is the key with which the meaning of the universe as a whole is unlocked. This is because the faith of Paul himself was cosmic in scope. You know, what the letter tries to say to us is what I have already tried to say. This Christ is bigger and more than we can ever imagine. How on earth we can put the petty limitations on him that we do I have no idea. How can we say that we know him fully or understand the ways that he works? Yet despite that we are intimately connected to the Lord. We are called together into a unity under Christ as the head and we are right at the centre of a universe being renewed by God.

That can sometimes be hard to see in a world that is often torn apart by violence and warfare but I think that is why we Christians are always called to see the bigger picture. God has a plan. The whole of the universe is being restored to its original harmony and completeness. Despite our wars and rumours of wars. Despite our inability to be in relationship with one another in peace and harmony. Despite the way injustice seems to reign all around us, God is leading us under Christ to a place of perfect unity. This new world has begun in the church as Christ's body but it goes way beyond the Church too.

The Church's role is to be a visible sign to the world of this new order where everything is connected and united. That means we have to be involved in Justice issues which cause so much division and disunity. Justice is not a side issue for the followers of Christ. We have no excuse for not being on the side of the little ones, those who hunger and thirst or those who are the victims of injustice. By standing for justice we reveal to the world the ultimate destiny of the whole of Creation.

We cannot stand for the renewal of the universe if we uphold unjust regimes or do nothing about the culture of death that is all around us. As Church, we have to stand for life from conception to natural death to counter that culture of death which is around us. John

Paul II in *Evangelium Vitae* said, 'We are facing an enormous and dramatic clash between good and evil, death and life, the 'culture of death' and the 'culture of life'. We find ourselves not only faced with, but necessarily in the midst of, this conflict; we are all involved and we all share in it, with the inescapable responsibility of choosing to be unconditionally pro-life.'

To be pro-life is not just a stance on abortion. It is a willingness to choose life in every situation. That is why it makes no sense to be anti-abortion and pro-death penalty. We stand for life or we do not. We stand for the rights of those who have learning difficulties and physical difficulties. We stand against human trafficking. We are on the side of life and that means we have to enter into the suffering of the world to help in the redemption of the world. Pope Francis at this time is calling the church to stand for justice and peace and there is opposition from those who do not see it as integral to the Church's mission. He has made many hard-hitting statements about the need for followers of Christ to be people of justice. One of them was this: 'Jesus tells us what the 'protocol' is, on which we will be judged. It is the one we read in chapter 25 of Matthew's Gospel: I was hungry, I was thirsty, I was in prison, I was sick, I was naked and you helped me, clothed me, visited me, took care of me. Whenever we do this to one of our brothers, we do this to Jesus.'

Caring for our neighbour; for those who are poor, who suffer in body and in soul, for those who are in need. This is the touchstone.' Without a stand for justice wherever we see injustice, we are failing in our mission to bring about the new creation that Christ died for.

I am not naïve and I know that having said all that, there are those who would point the finger at the Church itself and say 'practice what you preach.' I would be the first to acknowledge that there are issues in which as Church we need to develop our understanding. Sadly, the Church in the western world has become largely sterile and almost a club for the like-minded. We do not always live lives of faith, trusting that God is present with us and in our world. We make God fit our lives and our emotional realities and when God does not do that, we stamp our feet and do anything but trust in the overwhelming abundance that the Scriptures tell us that God is. Nor do we exhibit that overwhelming abundance for God in our stand against injustice. We need to reflect on some of the stances that we, as Church, take; which to many seem unjust and disrespectful of the dignity and value of the human person.

However, we also need to remember that we are a human institution and growth and change take a long time. We wait in joyful hope and anticipation for that development to take place. So we are called to stand for life and for justice at this time, in the best way we can, whilst always reflecting on our own need to change and develop. We are trying, with all our limitations, to be a sign to the world that the whole of creation is groaning and moving towards ultimate fulfilment.

This moving towards ultimate fulfilment that we are supposed to witness to is shown in the death of Christ on the cross. It is here that God shows us the lengths that God will go to in order to reconcile the world and to create the harmony that God desires. Never see Jesus' death on the cross as blood money. Rather it is the moment when we see who God is and how God loves in order to draw all things into unity. Our willingness to enter into the suffering in the world and bring reasons for living and hoping, is witnessing to that continuing reconciliation in Christ and the ultimate triumph of God. It is the drawing together of all things in him.

You see, what the Colossians and all of us are being challenged to become is Jesus himself, the sign of perfect unity. He was perfectly human with all the love compassion and mercy that implies. He was perfectly in relationship with the author of the universe and perfectly in relationship with all of the created order, the world and everyone who lives in it. The Colossians realised that they had begun to participate in a process of restoration intended by God. Each of them was to be recreated in God's own image, that is Christ, when they began to follow him. So they become Christ and share in his redeeming work, for the sake of the world. The same is true for us. We, who are responding to Christ, are called to be, in Christ, co-redeemers of the world.

Yes, it is done once and for all in time and space on Calvary but it is also outside time and space and therefore is a continual reality. The world has been transformed, is being transformed, and will be transformed. As Church, the body of Christ, we have a role to play in that transformation which leads to the ultimate unity of everything.

The early Christians seemed to understand that their lives were lived in God's own power. They also seemed to recognise that their struggle to transform the world through the power of good was in fact the activity of God. In this, Christ, the icon of God, was beginning the process of creation once again through the church. Do we have that sense that we are involved in the work of God? Are we aware that God is using us to re-create the world. Do we see every act of kindness and justice that we are involved in as being done in the power of God to bring about the ultimate reconciliation of the world with God and with itself? We will explore this as the chapter develops.

The author of Colossians is very clear that God had freely and lovingly chosen to dwell in human form in the person of Jesus Christ. This means not only that the fullness of God was present in Jesus but also that the fullness of God dwells in the Christ, whose body is the church in heaven and on earth. While we as individuals are transformed into Christ it is also together that we are a sign to the world. A phrase which for many years has meant a lot to our community in Southport is this: 'None of us has it all together but all together we have it all.' I think there is a challenge in that which we would do well to explore as we reflect on our call to be a visible sign of the presence of Christ in the world and the ultimate plan of God.

Many people these days have lost touch with institutional religion and seem to think that they can be Christian without being in relationship with others. I have heard people say, 'It is alright; I say my prayers but I do not need any Church.' It is a sort of anonymous Christianity. I can understand how that happens. It is easy to feel less than part of something that is huge or to feel misunderstood and hurt when an institution makes pronouncements that seem damaging to so many. Feelings of being let down, rejected, or abandoned, rise to the fore and it is easier to walk away than stay with the tension. Despite all of that we cannot go it alone. Tom Wright in his book on Colossians says this:

'It is undesirable and ultimately impossible for any individual Christian or Church to go it alone.'

It is together that we are the body of Christ. It is together we journey. It is together we work to create and witness to this new world order. Just because at times it is difficult to be part of the body is not an excuse not to be. If there are occasions when we do not agree with all the body says, that does not really give us an excuse to walk away. I remember watching a very moving and wonderful interview with Mary McAleese, the former Irish President. In it she very movingly spoke of her love for the Church and her desire to be part of the body of Christ. She was also very clear about some of the areas that were causing her difficulty. She got to the point in her reflection when she began to wonder should she stay within this church or should she walk away.

As part of her discernment she wrote to Pope John Paul II with her dilemma. One of his envoys wrote back to her urging her to remain within but not to compromise her conscience, simply to accept that her areas of disagreement were the church's teaching at this time. It was a powerful statement about remaining in relationship.

I guess the reason why the author of Colossians

understood our relationship with God and the world in this way is because of the contemporary philosophical understanding which was called Stoicism. Simply put, stoicism holds that the universe was considered to be a single body with a single rational spirit, which gave it life and order. For that reason all things were seen as parts of a whole. Everything affected everything else; nothing was random or isolated. Contemporary science might not accept that there is a single force that lies behind the cosmos; however science does accept that everything affects everything else. Everything is connected.

The author of the letter to the Colossians is obviously well aware of stoicism. That is why the use of the idea of the body of Christ to express the nature of the church is so apparent in the letter. Then the author of Colossians takes the idea forward another step. It seems there is a much bigger picture. That bigger picture, that the author of Colossians operates from, is the universe itself. The author of Colossians has been drawn into that bigger picture.

The author has begun to see that the church which is the body of Christ has cosmic dimensions, because the Christ of Colossians has cosmic functions. Jesus captures in time and space the truth of the cosmic Christ. What we see in him is true of the Christ who lives eternally. He is the lynch pin of God's plan for the whole of creation because in him everything is held together and reconciled. We, too, can see that our lives are part of that plan and that in us everything can be held together and seeming contradictions laid to rest. What a way to live!

In Colossians the author believes that Christian believers are part of a body of universal proportions. The Christ of which these ancient believers have become part is the fullness of God. We are caught up in the fullness of God, if we only had eyes to see. The whole of creation in all its glory is being called to reconciliation and unity which gives us hope to give our lives for the sake of those things. The whole of humanity, and all of creation, is offered a life free from bondage, sin, and despair. It is something that goes on deep within. I remember John McCarthy in his book *An Evil Cradling* saying of his Beirut captors, 'They can imprison my body but never my mind.' This is a freedom of mind and heart which enables us to enter into the bigger picture as we recognise that the whole of the created order is offered fulfilment and restoration under Christ. Paradise lost is restored. This bigger picture is such fantastic good news.

Ronald Rolheiser says this when reflecting on salvation, 'If Christ is the structure for the cosmic universe itself, the question of the normativeness of Christ for salvation

('There is no way to salvation, except through Christ.')
poses itself differently. The famous, early Christian
hymn in Ephesians speaks of 'a plan to be carried out
in the fullness of time to bring all things into one, in
Christ.' What's implied here, among other things, is
that Christ is bigger than the historical churches,
operates beyond the scope of historical Christianity
(although admittedly he does operate within it), and has
influences prior and beyond human history itself. It is
Christ, visible and invisible - the person, the spirit, the
power, and the mystery - who is drawing all things,
physical and spiritual, natural and religious, non-
Christian and Christian, into one.'

Within the universal framework of Colossians, what
does this mean? It means that if Christ has died, the
one who believes in him has also died. It means that if
Christ has been raised from the dead and now lives a
new life with God in heaven, so we too have been raised
up with Christ and live a new life in him. We stand for
the values of justice, truth, peace, love, forgiveness,
compassion, harmony, and unity. That is the new life
we have been given and it is real. It has been announced
in Christ to 'every creature under heaven' (Col 1:23). Is
that not extraordinary?

Many years ago, when a University Chaplain, I was
invited to dinner with a group of students. I was told

that they met once a month for support and sharing. It was a fascinating evening. These young people were both Christian and non Christian. They were all people of good will working around the city of Liverpool, in their spare time, to make a difference. They volunteered in soup kitchens, night shelters, and hospices. They worked with people who had learning difficulties and physical difficulties. They were involved in children's play schemes and worked in local schools and as prison visitors.

They were an extraordinary group of people and I felt very humbled by all they did. We ate together and then when the meal was finished there was a time of silence and at the end of that, each person in the room began to share their experience. It did not take very long for me to realise that what I was witnessing was the hidden life of Christ within these good people. Whether they saw it or not, for me it was a sign of the message of Christ drawing things together in peace and harmony. It filled me with hope and restored my belief in the ultimate destiny of the universe. I guess the question for us to reflect on is whether we believe that every good action is the hidden life of Christ coming to the fore. Then, of course, there is the decision, whether or not we allow that goodness to fill us with hope for the whole of the universe.

So the author of Colossians sees our identity as human beings in terms of the person and actions of Jesus Christ. As a member of Christ's body, we are secure in a threatening world because of the bigger picture that we hope and believe in, the ultimate plan of God for the whole of creation. The truth of salvation lives and grows within the church as long as it remains in contact with Christ as 'head'. This reality is offered to the world through our witness to unity, love, and harmony with all that entails. That sense of being safe, that we all want, is ours if we dare trust and believe in this abiding presence.

The Colossians believed in a Christ who was the source of their very existence and who is above all things and holds them in being. It is this Christ to whom they are connected as members of the church. They are being transformed into the image of this Christ for the world. By living out the realities in which it believes, the church can be the focus of a transformation of society.

It is possible that the peace and love, the mercy and forgiveness of God, can be seen in the world through us. This will always be an absolute and stark contrast to the disunity, strife, and self seeking that we still can experience every day on any street corner in any country in the world. It is an alternative to the hatred and suspicion, judgement and condemnation that are tearing the world apart. This way of living is a decision to view the world in a particular way. It is to face the world with a heart that is open, rather than with a heart which presumes badness rather than goodness. It is a way of embracing the world rather than separating oneself from it. All of that will witness to the bigger picture that all things are being drawn together into unity in Christ.

SIX

FATHER,
MAY THEY BE ONE

A few years ago I sat listening to a man tell his story to a couple of hundred people. It was a story of neglect, abuse, and the degradation of a child which led him to become a man who respected nobody, trusted nobody, and was deeply suspicious of goodness in any form. Chris was a violent angry man who turned to crime. Robbery, protection rackets, drugs and prostitution, were all part of his life. He was imprisoned time and again, which made him hate even more.

He was known throughout the Prison service as someone who was aggressive and who could only be controlled with force. He told us that he was so angry he would beat other prisoners up just so that he would be beaten up in turn. He was so badly damaged that he only felt fulfilled when someone else was pounding his face with their fists or kicking him hoping to do some real harm. He was moved from prison to prison in the hope of rehabilitation but nothing seemed to touch him.

He shared that within him there was an empty hole that nothing could fill, until he met a man who shared with him his faith. Chris' response was to beat him up and he almost killed him. He was placed in solitary confinement and when he came out of isolation the man came to him and shared his faith again and Chris reacted in the same way. Again he was carted away. The third time it happened Chris said he had to admire the man's tenacity. So he began to listen as the man told him the story of Jesus and who God is and Chris said that he began to weep and begged God to fill his need.

It took some time but Chris said his heart began to soften. It was not all plain-sailing though. There were still times when Chris got into trouble because he reacted with violence as he was used to doing and as people expected him to. Very slowly, however, he turned from his old way of life. He was released from prison and through a series of 'coincidences' found himself given a residential job looking after young people with special needs. His relationship with those children brought his healing to a conclusion.

At the end of his story he explained that now he lived in a small community where he ran a farm that sustained the community and what was left from the produce was given away to the poor. The people who work there have been in prison, have special needs, or are recovering addicts and Chris is the responsible person helping them and advising them and working with them to help them live their lives to the full.

He finished by quoting a line from Jean Vanier's book *Becoming Human*. 'We human beings are all fundamentally the same. We all belong to a common, broken humanity. We all have wounded, vulnerable hearts. Each one of us needs to feel appreciated and understood; we all need help.'

Under the skin we are all the same and, whether we recognise it or not, we are in relationship with God who is the creator of everything. We are in relationship with the world, which is gift, and we are in relationship with every human being who has ever walked the earth. The prayer for unity in John's Gospel is a prayer to discover the relational life that will heal us and transform us. The key to understanding this relational life is Jesus and so John in his Gospel simply explores the mystery that is God.

What I would like to try and do during this chapter is to put John 17 into that context, the context of relationship 'Father may they be one...' It is hugely important, for the sake of the world, that we find a way to move beyond the suspicious negativity that seems to be everywhere and a find a way of being one.

By the time we get to Chapter thirteen in the Gospel the pace is beginning to change. The Lord has worked his signs and people do not believe them. By and large they seem not to respond. He has shown them what it means to be a new creation, and again there is little positive response but plenty of negativity.

So by Chapter thirteen John has given up on telling us about signs and shows how real love can only be recognised through human action which is always a reflection, if a paltry one, of God's love. It seems as though John has begun to recognise that signs and wonders will not lead anyone into relationship with the Father. The only force to that is an experience of God's love at a human level. Remember, the word became flesh and is incarnate in each one of us. So we move into the Book of Glory, where we are drawn into that transfigured life to share the glory that Jesus has with the Father.

He shows us immediately who God is, by getting down on his knees and washing the feet of the disciples, and as always, there is resistance. Peter symbolises the Church that will not let God serve. Once again, John blows our image of God. We have to let God get down and wash our feet. It is an incredibly powerful image, it helps us realise that theologians and philosophers do not have all the answers to who God is. Jesus' response to that reticence is to say, 'If you do not let me wash your feet, you can have nothing to do with me.' It is topsy-turvy theology. John is telling us that we have to discover in our own experience the truth that Jesus is showing us in this action, a truth that turns everything upside down. You are loved by God.

When I was a child my mum had a friend called Kitty Verlin. Kitty was married to Bert who was a survivor of the first world war, a lovely warm gentle man who suffered greatly with ill health. He was constantly on oxygen and was never, as far as I remember, able to walk more than a few steps without struggling. Kitty's life was spent looking after Bert, responding to his needs cooking him delightful tasty meals in their tiny pensioner's flat. They had never had children and their lives were totally wrapped up in each other.

When Bert died Kitty was bereft. Her whole life had seemingly come to an end. After a few months, during which she was inconsolable, she began to realise that her life still had purpose and she decided that Bert would not want her to sit at home moping, so she dried her tears and put on her best hat and coat and went to see the Parish Priest.

Before long Kitty was cooking in people's houses around the Parish, preparing tasty meals, as she had for Bert, for those who were housebound. She baked and cooked and visited day in and day out. On Christmas eve she would make her special stuffing and would call at house after house, usually ending up in our kitchen peeling vegetables and stuffing the turkey. Her willingness to serve had huge benefits in Kitty's life as she became more and more loving. When she became too old to cook and bake and visit, people came to her because she radiated love and compassion and once she stopped 'doing' she was a valuable source of comfort and peace to many people until she died.

Kitty had learnt the lesson that if you have love to give you should give it and that serving people in ordinary ways was the way in which she was called to live out her life as a disciple. By doing that she became love. We are to wash the feet of those around us. It is the greatest sign of the presence of God.

That willingness to serve has its source in God. It is who God is for us, a willing servant, and to be caught up in the mystery that is God, we have to learn to be loving servants towards one another. The Gospel invites us to enter into the mystery of God and when we do that love and compassion happens within us and spills out from us. These wonderful values are not something we do but something we become when we enter into the mystery of God. We are love. We are compassion. We become Jesus. When you 'do' rather than 'are' you are one step removed from the mystery of God. We are to pour ourselves out so that others can find life.

In the next chapters Jesus talks about his departure and the future of the disciples. John simply walks around the mystery and repeats phrases and themes. That is why, intellectually, it is so confusing, and yet spiritually so enlightening. Someone was saying to me the other day that John's Gospel seems to say the same things over and over again. It does. It is John's way of exploring the mystery of God and of our relationship with God and with each other, walking around it again and again.

The farewell discourses begin in Chapter 13 verse 33 'My little children, I shall not be with you much longer.' We find a summary statement of what the next chapters are all about in verse 34. 'I give you a new commandment, love one another.' It is the beginning, the middle, and the end. It is everything. As I have passed on the Father's life to you, allow it to pass through you to others. Love is the only sign of the disciples of Jesus. It is not speaking in tongues, or being Catholic, or even being Christian, but love in every circumstance and the truth is that we cannot do it in our own strength.

At the beginning of Chapter fourteen we find Jesus responding to what is probably some of the fear that the disciples were feeling about the whole issue of love. It is almost as though in this action of the washing of the feet, a shaft of insight has penetrated their hearts. They have begun to see what it means to love and they do not know what to do.

Jesus says to them do not be worried, do not be frightened. We are to trust that the Lord is with us. It is almost as if he is saying, as you have faith in me and love me, the energy which is in me can begin to work in you. Right at the beginning of chapter 14 we find the desire of the lover is always to be with the beloved, the desire of Jesus is always to be with the disciples and that desire is timeless and so he says:

> 'I am going to prepare a place for you and after I have gone and prepared you a place I shall return to take you with me so that where I am you may be to.'

You can almost hear the frustration in Thomas who says, 'Lord, how can we know the way?' Jesus says, 'I am the way.' The way has become personal, It is not intellectual. He is the way, He is truth, He is life. It is all about relationship again. We define truth in terms of fact or right and wrong but truth is a person for John.

The Way is not just about the future but about the here and now. As we enter into relationship with 'I am' and the truth of 'I am' is awakened within us we will have come home, and that can never be taken from us. You will have discovered your true self and the God who gives you your true self. You might remember the verse from *Four Quartets* by T. S. Eliot which is quoted by Stephen Verney in his book on John's Gospel 'Water into Wine'

'We shall not cease from exploration and the end of all our exploring will be to arrive where we started and to know the place for the first time.'

It is another way of saying that our spiritual journey should make unfamiliar things familiar to us as we seek relationship with God, and therefore with all things.

Possibly even more importantly, it should make those things we take for granted new and unfamiliar. It is an invitation not to become comfortable with our lives and where we are in our lives. The only way to do this is to keep looking at our world through fresh eyes and to avoid the mind-numbing effects of our routines and habits. To have eyes that see rather than just look will always bring newness and freshness even to what we think we know. That's what real relationship does.

Philip then asks what is probably the desire of the heart of humanity, to see the Father. We find it expressed in many ways, in many fruitless searches, but that is the desire and John wants us to know that in seeing Jesus we have seen the Father.

We are called to believe in the moments when we have seen Jesus in the community and have been caught up in the love, tenderness, security, which reveals the Father to us. Moments that reveal to us eternity. Believe in those moments. Trust in them. If you do not trust in those moments how will you have faith to do the greater things that Jesus talks about? To go beyond yourself for the sake of others? Sadly, all too often we do not.

Jesus then reminds us that he will be with us, the advocate will come to be our defender. In Greek, the word is Paraclete. A Paraclete is one who stood by the little people who were unable to speak for themselves and fought their case in a court of law. Alfred, Lord Tennyson put it wonderfully in his poem *In Memoriam* when he said that we are:

> An infant crying in the night:
> An infant crying for the light:
> And with no language but a cry.

We are those little ones and the spirit of the absent

Jesus will be the Paraclete, to be with us and to help us as we face the world. We are not alone or alien because the Spirit is with us. That is how intimate the relationship is between us and this God.

He tells the disciples that the life-giving relationship that they have entered into will assure them of his life and his presence. Because of the life that is in them they will know that he is alive in them and they in him. What is the response to the knowledge of this indwelling love? Peace that the world cannot give or take away is the response.

Chapter fifteen is all about communion. It is about what it means to be present to another, to remain with another, it speaks of friendship. If you want to be a true friend read Chapter fifteen of John. You have to take the risk of intimacy, of knowing and being known, of being vulnerable and weak with someone else if you are to know how to be a friend. Somehow in entering into that sort of relationship with another person you will experience that sort of relationship with God. Why because God is present in the community. What is it like to be chosen, special, important? You will find it all in Chapter fifteen.

It is those sorts of relationships that will bear fruit, fruit that will last. The whole of the chapter is captured in the phrase, 'What I command you is to love one another'. It is an invitation to be constantly calling on his power, love, forgiveness, peace, so that we can be seen to stand in the name of Jesus as a sign of love in the world. We then find, at the end of Chapter fifteen the Paraclete, giving disciples the strength to be witnesses to the love of the risen Lord.

Chapter sixteen is almost like a re-run of fourteen as we begin to look again at the reality of the Spirit and the promise of the Spirits coming. The spirit will show us what sin is. The spirit will teach us what judgement is about, not our petty understanding, not vengeance or revenge but about love and life and respecting choice. The spirit will teach us as time goes on... 'there are many things that I still have to say to you but they would be too much for you now'.

It is a good lesson to learn, that there is a time for speaking and a time for keeping silent. It reminds us that evangelisation is a process because that is the way God deals with us: patiently, slowly, letting us build up our experience and our knowledge. Revelation is an ongoing process that never comes to an end. We move deeper and deeper in the mystery as time goes on. Christianity is not about verbalisation but about the experience of knowing the crucified Christ and recognising him, usually in the most broken and the poorest of the poor. I think it is so sad that we have made our Christian life all about words, dogmatic words and liturgical words. Relationship seems to be very much second best and yet it is the core of who and what we are.

The disciples then begin to understand and Jesus says that understanding will help them through their times of trial and misunderstanding in the world. He tells them that there will be trouble but to be brave because their experience of relationship with the Lord will sustain them. The advocate, the spirit, will carry them through to victory so do not be afraid.

What is he telling them is to choose now to believe that the victory is theirs. They have to choose now to believe that the circumstances of life that they have to face are not the sum total of everything. Life is not always going to be a bed of roses but, 'be brave, I have conquered the world'.

The same is true for us. Our relationship with the Lord is what will sustain us in times of difficulty. It is the spirit within us who will be there in the midst of trial and tribulation.

So we move into Chapter seventeen. In Chapter eleven we had a statement that Jesus came to gather the scattered children of God into unity. Here we have the unpacking of what that means. Unity is the work of God. Everything up to this point has been about unity, unity with God in intimate relationship, unity with one another through service, unity with creation respecting and loving it.

The farewell speeches of the great men often ended with a prayer of protection for their followers and for their teaching to be lived out in them. This is Jesus' farewell speech and his prayer that his teaching be lived out within those who follow him.

In it he pulls together all the strands of his life together. He tries to show them all that he has believed in, and all that he has held dear, he wants his followers to hold dear as well.

We find John stating again that real life only comes through knowing Jesus in the intimate way that the word 'knowing' meant for the Hebrews. It is all about relationship. If only we would believe that life comes through knowing Jesus and that we are invited to enter into the glory of the family of God, to allow God to possess us, envelop us so that we can find life, love and peace.

He then prays for that unity between believers that will

sustain and guide them and that his Disciples might really live in the world. We are not called to be removed from the world but to live in it and enjoy it. So many Christians seem to think that we have to avoid the world and hide away from it. That seems to me a false understanding. Read the words from the Gospel... 'I am not asking you to remove them from the world.' If you want a safe, cosy, haven to escape from the rigours of life, Christianity is not for you.

The world is not a bad place, It is God's gift to us, but we are chosen to show other people the gift that it is when it is loved and lived in with respect. Our vocation as human beings is to really enter into the world with all its beauty and magnificence and to live in it in the way God intended us to live. In order to do that we are asked to move beyond the superficial level that most people live at, asking ourselves deep questions about how we live with one another and with creation.

Over the last few years I have become very aware of the phrase that, for the Gospel to happen amongst us, it has to first of all happen within us. The primary place for any transformation to happen has to be within. If we are to live out the call to be a chosen people helping others to understand that they too are chosen then we have to allow the spirit of God to free us from the false understanding of humanity, life and the world that we are bound to have.

So that transformative process starts deep within us, with the letting go of so much that we gather through life, which does not allow us to grow in relationship. We have to be honest, sometimes brutally so. We all have to face things like false perceptions of humanity and sour cynicism about life and the world. We have to deal with, and let go of, critical judgemental approaches to everyone and everything that dogs so many of us.

During the process we are slowly freed from suspicion about one another. We begin to face the world with a heart that is open, rather than a heart which is wary or a heart that is mistrustful. As the spirit works deeply within us we find ourselves choosing to view the world and life in a particular way, presuming goodness rather than badness. We become loving, merciful, compassionate, free human beings. That way of living and being is our witness to the truth of humanity and the beauty of the world.

Jesus then goes on to pray for unity. It is a call to us to live our lives for the sake of unity. The world cannot produce unity. Only the presence of God can draw us into unity. If you want to live a fully Christian life then give your life for unity, for relationship. That will shatter your political ideologies, your social ideologies; it will revolutionise the way that you live and your understanding of life. In verse 26 we find that love is the force that can make unity and this entering fully into the world a reality, but it is Divine love.

The prayer parallels the 'Our Father' in the synoptic Gospels in that it is addressed to the Father and it is prayed that the father be glorified, hallowed, here. It is concerned that the kingdom come on earth and that the disciples be protected from the evil one.

Unlike the 'Our Father' it is not a teaching on how to pray but an invitation to enter into prayer with the Father and the Son. It is an invitation into relationship with them. It is a glimpse of the intimacy between them and a reflection of the love that they have for us, in allowing us to share in that intimacy. When Jesus prays that we be one, all that this chapter contains and far more is behind that prayer. If we take the prayer seriously it will catapult us into a life that is rich and full and always surprising. It will be deeply challenging but ultimately fulfilling, as we realise the truth that it is all about relationship, mirroring God who is perfect relationship.

SEVEN

WE ARE ONE

A long time ago in my teenage years I used to spend a lot of time in Dublin. The memories I have of the wonderful people I met there during that time, remain with me today. I often think of the community around Sallynoggin and further afield and the laughter and the fun we had. They taught me much about the Gospel and about the willingness to give everything for the sake of the Gospel, something I still struggle with each day.

One day I decided to surprise my friends and jumped on a boat to Dublin. In those days you could be a foot passenger for round about ten pounds. It was a particularly rough crossing and I had slept all night on the floor in a bin bag. It was difficult to avoid the pools of vomit and so when we docked the next morning I was not smelling my most fragrant! I got off the boat to find there was a bus strike and so thumbed a lift out to Glenageary.

When I arrived there I found the three families that I knew well were all away. In my naivety I had not thought to get in touch and find out if it was okay for me to come. One of the neighbours told me that some of my friends would be back the next day but there would be no one there that night. I really did not know what to do so I hung around for a while and eventually got a lift back into Dublin.

Sadly I did not have a lot of money with me and was not able to afford to stay anywhere. I spent part of the night wandering around Phoenix park. I was terrified, convinced that I was going to get beaten up and maybe even murdered. Whenever I settled down on a bench I kept getting moved on. So I eventually decided that I would go back into the city centre. I went to the Cathedral and then eventually I sat down not too far from there.

After a while I was joined by a man who told me that he was called Michael. I had settled down on his plot but he was not angry with me for getting there first. He said that he always stayed in this spot over night because it was safe and then he did something amazing. He shared what little food and drink he had with me and we spent the night talking and laughing and dozing till about five o'clock in the morning, when he decided it was time for him to move on. I stayed another couple of hours and then went to the first Mass in the Cathedral. Eventually I managed to get out again to Glenageary where I found some of my friends had returned and I was given a typical warm Irish welcome.

I have never forgotten Michael and was so grateful to this man of the road who shared a few hours of his life with me and his little bit of food. It made me realise a truth that I have discovered on many occasions since that under the skin we really are all the same. Whether we like it or not we are part of creation. We share a common unity with every human person. We are all born into this world graced by God and created by God. We are not put into this world to live divided from one another by race, creed, sexuality, skin colour, or language.

We are not meant to live separately from one another but together to try to find meaning in this stage of our existence that we call humanity. In fact, what we tend to do, is live in isolation from one another, full of fear and anxiety about the other. What we seem to do is make difference a source of disunity rather than searching together for meaning. We justify it by quoting our religions and taking political stances when really all we are doing is protecting ourselves and refusing to move into the bigger picture where we live our lives for the sake of humanity and the collective reality that we are.

In a letter to a man who had lost his young son to polio,

Albert Einstein once wrote, 'A human being is part of the whole called by us 'the universe,' a part limited in time and space. He experiences himself, his thoughts and feelings, as something separated from the rest, a kind of optical illusion of his consciousness. The striving to free oneself from this delusion is the one issue of true religion. Not to nourish the delusion but to try to overcome it is the way to reach the attainable measure of peace of mind.'

I was recently talking to a man from Romania who sells the Big Issue not too far from where I live. He told me that since the referendum on Europe, he was constantly being taunted by groups of young people. They were telling him he would soon be going home and he had no place in this country. As he shared with me the tears were tripping down his face and I could not help but feel a deep sense of shame that we have come to this.

Whatever stance you might have taken on our place in Europe, the Gospel invites us always to be compass-ionate, loving and on the side of those in need. Not to take that stance, even in these troubled times, is to be less than faithful to the call of the Gospel. It can never be right to be, through anger and bitterness, exultant at another's misfortune, which is the experience my Romanian friend is having.

It strikes me that in the heart of God there is no room for separation or division. God is perfect unity and we as individuals and community are made in the image and likeness of God. The blame, separation and scapegoating that seems to govern the world are not a true reflection of what it means to be a human being. We should be co-operating with one another, rejoicing in difference and sharing our common humanity. So how can we let suspicion and fear rear its ugly head? How can we let struggles for power, jockeying for position, and wanting our own way destroy the simple call to be united in love? How can we create camps of the like-minded that become exclusive rather than inclusive when all the time that fails to reflect the true nature of humanity which is to be at one?

I guess that is why I think we need to hear again this call to unity, to come together and do as much as we possibly can to stand against the scandal of disunity. That will change our image of God. There is only one God. It will challenge us deep within as we have to let go of our need to be right and for others to be wrong. It will call us into relationship with others who see things differently but it will bring us and others life and we will, without doubt, be true to the nature of humanity made in the image and likeness of God.

What is that truth? It is that we are fantastic people.

Throughout Scriptures you find wonderfully moving statements of what it means to be a human being. The book of Genesis reminds us that we are made in the image and likeness of God. The Psalms tell us that we are fearfully and wonderfully made, that we are clothed with dignity and honour, we are little less than a God and that we are crowned with glory and splendour. Statement after statement that reminds us of the dignity of every human person.

St Paul speaks beautifully of the wonder of humanity when he writes 'you are God's work of art', or again, 'you are a temple of the Holy Spirit.' He very brilliantly says 'you are filled with the utter fullness of God.' Who, me? Filled with the fullness of God? How extraordinary that makes humanity. We are told that we are 'God's chosen race,' Of course that does not just apply to those of us who are faith filled people but to those who are not people of faith, those who have not yet been able to discover those truths.

Many years ago I went to lead a retreat somewhere on the South Coast with a semi-enclosed group of sisters. I was told that there were fifteen in the community and that all the sisters would be involved in the retreat. At the first session there were only fourteen and then again at the second and third. Eventually I asked about the missing nun and was told that Sister Augusta never came out of her room.

Typically of me, I let my imagination run riot with all sorts of images of the crazy nun locked in the attic who roamed the building at night with a knife in her hand. Eventually I was asked to go and see Sr Augusta and I was terrified. It is amazing what you can allow the mind to conjure up.

I was led down several corridors and eventually was face to face with a huge door. The sister who was with me knocked and a voice called out 'come in' and in we went. I have to say the fact that the door was not locked did a lot to ease my fears.

I went in and there was Sister Augusta kneeling by her bed. She turned and stood facing me with a rosary in her hand and it was clear she was not very well. In fact she was tortured. As she talked to me I realised that she was convinced that she did not pray enough, had not been good enough during her life and that she was going to hell. She was terrified, not recognising that she was already living in the hell that so frightened her. She stayed in her room so that she would not sin further.

I felt so sad when I met her because she had no sense of her own dignity or the wonder of her being. She did not know any those things that the Scriptures speak of as being true for her. The religion that she had given her life to had in fact stopped her believing that she was wonderful So this woman lived a fractured, broken existence in a small dark room without any hope. If only she could have understood how wonderful she really was. If only she knew the truth of the many statements in the Scriptures and in the Church documents her life would have been so different.

As I reflect on those statements I am filled with gratitude and wonder. We human beings are all filled with the possibility of potential and creativity whatever our colour, creed, or sexuality. We can all fly within, according to our potential. At the same time I am filled with horror when I see what our disunity does to our brothers and sisters. Is it right that some should be denied that possibility for the fulfilment of potential because of the greed of others or the petty moralising of others? Is it not possible for us to learn to live for the common good rather than for what we think is our own good?

I think part of our faith journey has to be the willingness to let go of the labels we put on people and our theories about what is right and wrong. This is a huge challenge. We have to face that insidious racism, sexism, and homophobia that seems to be lurking just under the surface. I think most of the time we are not even aware of its existence but in order to recognise our common humanity and live to promote that unity we have to face the truth and let go of our often unjustified prejudices.

The other day, I was celebrating Mass in a local Church and afterwards a man I knew well came in and asked another Parishioner what the name of the African Priest was, who was coming to them for the Summer. When he was told Patrick, he burst out laughing and made some comment about that not being a very African name. Now he is not a bad man and will be welcoming and polite to Patrick but there was something going on under the surface that he just did not see. There is so much letting go and so much need to simply ponder, reflect, and pray about what goes on within us regarding those who are different from us. Take time to notice what is and simply hold it.

Why would we do this? I think when we become aware of what is within us without condemning ourselves then we become more open to the possibility of trans-formation. When transformation starts to happen within us we will in time become so aware of the mystery of God's presence that we will rejoice at that presence in every human being. It is then that we will come to know the truth that we are called to live for the sake of humanity and for the unity of humanity.

One of the most extraordinary people I have ever met is Jean Vanier, the founder of L'Arche and the Faith and Light movements. I remember standing with him at a gathering of several hundred people. When he looked at anyone it was as though that person was the only person in the world. He had an extraordinary ability to be present to another human being and the respect and the love that one could see in his eyes was truly inspirational. It's obvious that his amazingly profound and deep contributions to our understanding of 'being human' are informed by his deep faith and his philosophical training.

More than that, I think it would be fair to say, that his main inspirations are the transformative experiences of sharing life with people who have a disability. In his book *Becoming Human* he writes, 'We human beings are all fundamentally the same. We all belong to a common, broken humanity. We all have wounded, vulnerable hearts. Each one of us needs to feel appreciated and understood; we all need help.'

Faith should deepen our understanding of our common identity. It should open our minds up and help us see more clearly. It is certainly not meant to make us more parochial and more narrow. Faith moves us from that place where it is all about me to a place of broad vision in which everything has a place and belongs.

You know sometimes we can be the narrowest, hardest, prejudiced, intolerant people you could ever care to meet. It is true within every major religion, Islam, Christianity, Hinduism, and Buddhism. It is a reality within different Christian traditions, within Catholicism, Methodism, Anglicanism and more. We spend a lot of time scapegoating, blaming, and judging others often without recognising that we are indulging in this without even being aware. What was it Jesus said?... 'Take the log out of your own eye before taking the speck out of your brother's or sister's eye.

I remember watching a Louis Theroux programme some years back. It was about the intolerance of some Christian groups against gay people. I was horrified to hear some of those interviewed say that every human person who was attracted to others of the same sex should be chemically castrated or executed. We have a lot to learn from Jesus and his way which is always about love and compassion and the holding of each soul with tenderness.

In the fourth century, St. Augustine said that the church exists in the state of communion of the whole world. What was he trying to say? I think it is something like this, that wherever we are in right relationship, wherever we are loving, compassionate, forgiving and welcoming there is the church. I have seen 'Church' in soup kitchens, self help groups, vaulted cathedrals and coffee shops. God is always bigger and more and can be found everywhere if we care to look.

Sadly, over the years Christians whittled that Great Mystery down into something small, exclusive, and manageable. The church became a Catholic, Orthodox, or Protestant private club. It was not necessarily formed by people who were aware of their common identity with the natural world, with non-Christians, or even with other Christians outside their own denomination.

Richard Rohr says that salvation 'became a very tiny salvation, hardly worthy of the name.' God became small and manageable and could only be found where we presumed God could be found. Much of what we did and do as Church is about us and our need to fulfil our own ego rather than being about God and the neglected call to recognise our common brotherhood and sisterhood.

That is why I love the documents of the Second Vatican Council because they correct that narrowness and push us out towards the world. I will quote them often in this book because they invite us to look for common purpose and meaning and reflect on them in the light of the Gospel. Sadly I do not think many Catholics have read the documents. Nor do many know that a Vatican Council is the highest form of Church teaching. It cannot be undone. It can only be developed.

There is one document, in particular, from the council that shattered my understanding about what it really means to be a Catholic Christian when I first read it. It is called *Gaudium et Spes* or 'The Church in the Modern world' and in it are the most incredibly moving statements about humanity. It talks of the dignity of the human person and the basic goodness within the human person. It reflects beautifully on the ultimate destiny of the human person and our final resting place in the mystery that is God.

It has in it quotations like this, 'This Council lays stress on reverence for the human person; all people must consider their every neighbour without exception as another self, taking into account, first of all, life and the means necessary to living it with dignity.'

Every human being, the people we work with, the people we pass on the street have both a dignity and a destiny that can never be taken from them. I have often written that John Paul II said that every human being has the spark of the divine within them even if they do not know it. If you discover that for yourself then you will begin to discover it everywhere.

When you know the truth that God sees you as wonderful then you will begin to see every human person as wonderful, whether they be Moslem, Hindu, Christian, or of no faith at all.

It is then that mercy becomes the deepest part of you. It is not something you do but something that you are because of your awareness of the love of God for everyone. It fashions you at the core of your being and you live life with nothing to protect because all is good at its core and there is nothing to be afraid of.

When we know in the depths of our being the marvel and wonder of humanity then we do not need to protect ourselves from other human beings. Rather, we begin to see the need to break down barriers. We see that we do not need to be fearful and anxious we need to be merciful. We discover that we do not need to be narrow, suspicious and closed. Instead we can be open and welcoming. Why? Because every human person is the same as we are. Every human person is our brother and our sister. It seems to me, that what Christian faith says to us, is that love and service of our brothers and sisters are at the core of what it means to be human, that hospitality and welcome are supposed to be our key attributes.

A few months ago I was listening to a programme on

the television and the title of the part of the programme I was watching was, 'Does the Catholic Church need to change?' One of the panellists on it was a theologian and a member of a Religious order. Whenever she was faced with a difficult question by the host she simply smiled and said 'whoever loves lives in God and God lives in them'. Love is the litmus test of what it means to be a human being and is always a deep sign of the presence of God. I often think to myself that God is in many places that the Church cannot or will not acknowledge.

God took the initiative with love, love that shows us we are forgiven and redeemed in the person of Jesus. That is at the heart of the Gospel, a God who has always loved humanity, who has forgiven humanity from the very moment of creation, a God who desires intimacy with us. I would want to say that Jesus simply reveals the heart of God, shows us who God has always been. It is the most amazing incredible Good News.

Since God has loved us in such a way the author of the first letter of John repeats again and again that we are to love one another in order to be of God. You see it is all about love and service and welcome and unity and acceptance.

This Gospel is not just about personal relationship with

the Lord, it also forces us into relationship with other people. We are called to know love and to share love, and love, real love, is indiscriminate. We are called to love everyone regardless of colour, creed, sexuality, gender. So the core of what it means to be Christian is also the core of what it means to be human.

The beautiful encyclical written by Pope Francis called *Laudato Si* has made me more and more aware that the one thing we have in common, which may just bring us together, is the planet we live on and the mess that it is in. The earth and its life systems, on which we all entirely depend, might soon become the very thing that will convert us to a simple lifestyle, to necessary community, and to an inherent and universal sense of reverence for that which is holy.

We all breathe the same air and drink the same water. We all need the same things to live. There are no Jewish, Christian, or Muslim versions of these universal elements. Together we have to find a way of living in peace and harmony and surely that begins with a recognition of our common humanity, which in turn means we have to let go of our narrowness and begin to love and respect every brother and sister.

I read recently that 'surrendering to love is what we are all called to do everyday of our lives.' Jesus was so right when he said that the greatest commandment was to love God and our neighbour as ourselves. Victor Frankl who suffered through the Nazi concentration camps and survived wrote, 'Love is the ultimate and highest goal to which man can aspire. The salvation of man is through love and in love.'

Surrender to love today. Make the decision to love God. Make the decision to love yourself. Make the decision to love everyone as yourself. God is Love and every human person is a product of that extraordinary love. To learn to love regardless of the differentials we put on each other is to co-operate in God's plan of salvation for the whole universe.

EIGHT

Unity Within

My friend Helen, who lives many miles away from me and whom I see very seldom, has had a profound effect on my life. Helen is bi-polar, at least that is what the doctor's say. There are times when she is very high and times when she is very low. When she is high she goes to extremes, spending huge amounts of money booking holidays and buying cars. When she is low she can hardly get out of bed and struggles to put one foot in front of the other.

There have been times in Helen's life when she has been arrested for her behaviour in public and sectioned under the mental health act. Boundaries have always been difficult for Helen and that has led her into many sticky situations. She has trusted people that she should never have, and not trusted those she should. I think it would be fair to say that life has been a roller coaster of a ride for her.

These days Helen is a much calmer person. Her medication helps but so does her self awareness, which has increased dramatically. She long ago gave up condemning and judging herself for who she is and accepts herself with all the difficulties of her personality. She knows her triggers and avoids stressful sessions. She laughs at herself constantly and is probably one of the most rounded whole human beings I know. She has taught me about acceptance and love of self in a way that few others have.

I think it is true to say that we are probably fairly fragmented people and that most of us struggle towards wholeness. Within Christian circles many people that I talk to think that wholeness is about perfection. It is then presumed that the journey is about getting rid of what we call weakness and vulnerability. I think that has been much of the basis of our spirituality and it is a very muscular approach to Christianity. Change yourself and get rid of imperfection. I do not believe that any more, if I ever did. I sometimes think the secular world has a much better handle on what it means to be an integrated human being than many Christians have, as we wrestle with ourselves and see so much of what we call 'sin' within.

I came across this recently from David Benner in a journal called 'Oneing' which expresses beautifully what I think is true. 'Spare me perfection. Give me instead the wholeness that comes from embracing the full reality of who I am, just as I am. Paradoxically, it is this whole self that is most perfect. As it turns out, wholeness, not perfection, is the route to the actualisation of our deepest humanity.

Inconsistencies, imperfections, and failures to live up to ideals are all part of what it means to be human. What seems to distinguish those who are most deeply and wholly human is not their perfection, but their courage in accepting their imperfections. Accepting themselves as they are, they then become able to accept others as they are.'

It is a huge challenge to accept yourself as you are and to rejoice in who you are. It seems that most of us want to reject that which is weak and vulnerable, presuming that those things are not what a whole person experiences. I think those things are precisely what a whole person experiences. I often think of the appearances of the risen Christ who showed the disciples the wounds in his hands and his feet. The risen Christ is still the wounded one. Who would dare say that he was not a fully rounded human being?

Benner goes on to say 'The richness of being human lies precisely in our lack of perfection. This is the source of so much of our longing, and out of that longing emerges so much creativity, beauty, and goodness. With appropriate openness and humility, it is the cracks that let in the light. Once those cracks and flaws are embraced and accepted as part of the self, then, and only then, can the light flow out though them, into the lives of others and into the world.

For a couple of years I was quite ill with depression. It came from a place of deep brokenness, which began in my childhood and which is still part of me. I had to face a lot of pain and accept that I could not change what had happened to me or the damage it had caused. What I could do was to accept it and let it become a gift. As I try to do that I hope I have become more compassionate, more loving, and more accepting of others.

Carl Jung said that 'The privilege of a lifetime is to become who you truly are.' Wounds, brokenness, vulnerability can help you to become who you really are. They can make you a more rounded and open human being, more open to the needs of others, more accepting and understanding of others ways. I think you can become, in time, what Henri Nouwen calls 'a wounded healer.'

I love the Scriptures and I think that the Scriptures are constantly inviting us to enter into the mystery of what it means to be a fully rounded human being, an integrated person. Sadly most of us treat them as only historical stories, which causes all sorts of problems as we wrestle with the scourge, and very real danger, of fundamentalism. In many senses they are a reflection on the human journey and the interaction between the human and the divine. The Historical perspective, whatever that may be, takes second, third or even fourth place to that journey. So from beginning to end the Scriptures invite us into a place of vulnerability where we are not in control, where we do not have all the answers. It is a place where life is about journeying and discovering, trusting, risking, letting go, and living. The Scriptures lead us to into a real earthy human reality, where we know the truth that God is in all things, even the mess. There has probably been a lot of mess in all our lives, and salvation and redemption are all about being at peace with who we are. The fantastic experience of loving self can change us deeply and life can become vibrant and full as God meant it to be.

Many years ago when I was working as a youth Chaplain I used to take groups of young people to Kintbury in Berkshire, a De La Salle house, where they experienced the 'Kintbury diamond'. It was simply a piece of paper on which was drawn a diamond shape. The page was divided into four parts and the young people had to list in each section qualities they liked about themselves, and then some they did not like; talents they had and areas where they could make changes. In the middle of the diamond was written, 'I am okay because God does not make rubbish'.

God did not make a mistake in making us as earthly physical beings. We are created to love our physicality. We are filled with wonderful powerful, creative energies which cause us to be always searching and looking for life. We are created as social, relational beings, filled with deep physical hungers that are meant to be fulfilled and enjoyed. That is the reality of our human condition. It is who we are, and how we are meant to be, and God does not make rubbish. The sooner we get in touch with ourselves, and all that is within us, and begin to live, the better.

Sadly, most of us condition ourselves to not being real about what is going on within our lives not just with other people but with ourselves. We pretend rather than face the human reality. We seem to be afraid of our inner life and our vulnerability and so try and act as if it does not exist.

I learnt that very powerfully when I did my family tree and discovered lots of stories from my family's background. One such story is that of Elizabeth Pring who was my great great grandmother. I had been to Israel with a group of people and returned to find a message on the answer phone telling me that one of my second cousins had been looking through some old documents of her mother's and grandmother's. In the course of looking through them she had come across an old letter from some relative or another telling the story of the said Elizabeth.

Elizabeth had been born in the 1820's into a fairly well off family. They lived in a big house in Cheshire and had servants and gardeners and obviously a very nice life-style, at whose expense I hardly dare think. Elizabeth had fallen in love with one of the gardeners and was discovered with him in the greenhouse. Her father sacked the gardener on the spot, dragged Elizabeth back to the house and locked her in her room.

Each night the gardener would appear at the gate to the house in the hope of seeing Elizabeth. She eventually escaped from the house and ran away with him. They lived in very poor circumstances, hardly any money and lots of children on the scene. Elizabeth tried on several occasions to make contact with her father but he refused to see her. He never communicated with her again, disowned her, and cut her out of his will. She never spoke of any of this to her family and it was as though it had never happened.

The letter then went on to say how when Elizabeth was

a very old lady, she told her story to her family. She had very successfully built up walls about her sad life and for many years she had simply pushed away the pain of rejection. However it had its effect and the letter said that she was a bitter, angry woman not at peace with herself at all and when she told her story, her family finally understood why.

As the epic story unfolded it was as though the floodgates opened and the walls of protection began to crumble. She cried about her father's stubbornness and the sense of rejection she had felt. She cried about the loss of her sisters and her mother. It seemed that as she cried she found a new freedom and was able to experience deep within herself, a peace that she had never had. She visited her father' and mother's grave and laid wreaths laying her ghosts to rest.

Having done this, the letter said that Elizabeth was very much at peace, in a way that she had never known before. She said that she had experienced deep healing and reconciliation within herself. All of it because she had stopped pretending and faced herself, allowing healing to happen.

I have said on many occasions that the good news of the Gospel is that God loves us as we really are with a radical overwhelming love that we can only ever glimpse. The good news of Jesus Christ is that we do not have to be perfect to be loved. Remember David Benner's words 'spare me from perfection'. Our vulnerability and brokenness will never stop God loving us, nothing can ever do that.

Challenge any image of God that you might have picked up during your life that would tell you that God is not wonderfully loving. It does not matter what you were taught as a child about God. Begin again and dare to believe in the overwhelming power of love which allows us to be fully who we are without condemnation. 'For God so loved the world that he sent his only son not to condemn the world but so that through him the world might be saved.' To dare to believe in the God who has risked everything to sanctify the whole of humanity can free us to love ourselves as we realise that in God's eyes we are wholly and completely wonderful.

We cannot earn salvation by trying to be perfect. Wholeness and integration comes when we accept and love who we are, warts and all. If that is not a lived experience of salvation then I do not know what is. Let the love of God flow through you so that you can know who you are and begin to live life.

That sense of love frees us to have the courage to explore ourselves and to experience and accept the truth

of who we are. It is then that we can begin the process
of letting go, knowing the truth that God is with us,
freeing us, calling us to life, leading us to wholeness
and integration Once we know that we do not have to
earn God's love, that everything is gift, then we can
begin to respond to the invitation that the Scriptures
give us to become fully human and fully alive.

If we are honest, there is so much to let go of on this
journey towards wholeness and integration of ourselves.
It is easy to say this, but so much harder to put into
practice. Let go of the anxiety about what you see as
your shortcomings and recognise that they might well
be your greatest gift. It is a battle of the mind and a
challenge to our perceptions as much as it is anything
else. Try and hold the tension of your own reality
without putting a value judgement on it. Let go of your
sensitivity towards yourself and what you see as good or
bad within you. Do not demonise yourself.

Many years ago I met a young woman called Sharon
whose life, as she saw it, was a mess. She had four
lovely children, a good lifestyle with lots of friends
and a good supportive family. She was a well motivated
business woman with three dress shops. Yet she was
consumed by guilt and anxiety over minor mis-
demeanours. She was terrified about anybody really
knowing what she was like and told me over and over

again that she hated herself. She could see nothing good within. As far as she was concerned she was a bad mother, a bad wife, a bad daughter, and a terrible business woman who was going to go bust and put lots of people out of work. None of it was true but she believed it to be so. She had demonised herself and could not break free. Eventually she tried to take her own life and was hospitalised.

It took years of psychotherapy and counselling to help Sharon move away from her self-condemnation. It took a long time for her to even begin to accept that the way she saw things was maybe a little bit skewed to say the least. Now, thank God, she has begun to accept her frailty, vulnerability, and her emotional life without condemning herself and for Sharon there has begun to be a glimmer of light at the end of the tunnel.

I have written about this before but this call to wholeness and integration means that we have to let go of the masks we wear, the games we play, the hurts we hold on to, in order to struggle towards wholeness. Try and find a trusted friend with whom you can share yourself. I am very lucky in my life to have two or three, and one in particular, very close people, with whom I can share the grittiness and rawness of my own struggle. It is incredibly freeing to have someone accept, without judgement, who you are, and love you regardless of what you share.

Recently I was giving a retreat and the conversations I had made me realise again that the power of our emotions are the source of much of our fear about who we are. How can I be a good Christian, a follower of Jesus when I am angry and hurt? How can I live the Gospel when I have within me jealousy and frustration? How can I be the face of Christ when I am weak and vulnerable? How do I follow the Lord when I have within me passions and creativity that I find difficult to harness?

Our emotionality, but more our response to it, can really do a job on us if we reject and push away who we are and what is within us. Our acceptance of it all can powerfully set us free so that we are no longer held in thrall by what goes on within and we can begin to know that because of what we experience we have a much richer and deeper life and much more insight into humanity.

I think we have to have the courage on this journey towards wholeness and integration to process what goes on within us. There is also a need to accept what we find within or we simply dump it all on to those around us. We become people who blame, accuse, and attack others for what we hate within ourselves. If we do not become someone who blames and attacks, it is possible that we become abusive control freaks, forcing people to do what we want just to make ourselves feel better. One of the areas that can wound us very badly is the area of sexuality. In fact it is probably the root of much of our emotional damage. It is very hard to accept God does not frown on us when we are so motivated by our sexuality, which for generations we have seen as wrong or evil at the worst and at the best flawed and a bit damaged. It seems as though all of us are either guilt based or shame based people.

Henry Nouwen once described evil in human beings as our endless capacity for self-rejection and self-destruction. Sadly, many people constantly berate themselves for their sexuality and for what are considered to be our baser feelings. It is usually because of poor teaching from well meaning Priests and sisters who were terrified of sin and saw sexual sin as worse than any other.

Why sexual 'sin' was, and is still, seen by many as being worse than any other I do not really know, other than much of the perceptions of Priests and Religious came from a misunderstanding of Paul who was seen to frown on anything to do with the body. They also came from St Augustine whose own lifestyle and subsequent conversion from it led him to see things in a particular way.

To be passionate is very human and very wonderful. It is not bad or wrong. God created us as passionate, sexual beings. Of course, like everything else, we can misuse it but it is a good and wholesome reality. We have to rediscover that truth and let go of the false teachings that so many of us were given about sexuality. Sexuality is in many senses the energy of life and is much more than just sleeping with someone as the culture of the day would tell us. Integrated human beings are able to love their sexuality as the energy within them that causes delight and wonder.

One of the realities that we all have to face is that we do not know everything. More than that to realise that what we think we know can change and develop over generations. I think that means we have to always remain open to newness in the way that we see things and never to presume that the last word has been spoken about anything. I am always amazed how we manage to make our little part of history, our lives, the only reality there is. We certainly do it in the Church. Do something twice and it becomes tradition, do it three times and it becomes dogma! While that has benefits there have been huge developments in the area of sexuality in recent years that it would be wise for us to reflect on and be open to.

I guess the most whole human being who ever lived

was Jesus. Ronald Rolheiser reflects on the humanity of Jesus and quotes some research done by Philip Cunningham who wrote a book on Jesus that he called: *A Believer's Search for the Jesus of History*. What Philip Cunningham does is to gather together and reflect on much of the recent work that has been done about the actual person of Jesus. What was Jesus like? What kind of person was he?

In the book the author suggests that the wonderful phrase at the end of the infancy narratives in Luke's Gospel "He increased in wisdom and in years, and in divine and human favour,' helps us to get an insight into what he was like. He was obviously very much rooted in his culture which probably meant that he had an ordinary family upbringing, was part of a community, and just got on with living.

It's obvious from the Scriptures that he must have had a very healthy upbringing because when he began his ministry, he knew how to share food with people. He was able to banter with those he came in contact with. He was not frightened to argue his point of view. He could tell challenging stories par excellence, laced with humour and irony. He went to parties and drank wine and laughed and talked. He understood the joys and tragedies of life. His preaching, with its vitality and authenticity, shows that he was able to value intimacy, friendship, community, and enjoyment. He was able to enjoy life that scandalised the religious authorities of his day. He related to women and outsiders and sinners in ways that a good Jew would not do. He had an extraordinary ability to forgive and be compassionate towards people regardless of whether they were a Roman soldier, a paralysed man or even a thief hanging next to him on the cross.

Several years ago a religious sister gave me a picture which was called the laughing Jesus. It is a wonderful picture of Jesus with his head thrown back roaring with laughter, unable to conceal the delight within him. It shows the all too human Jesus who understood the gift that life is and who heard the call to live it to the full.

Rolheiser captures it beautifully when he says that he, Jesus, was a man of 'resilience, hope, faith, forgiveness, capacity for enjoyment, sense of humour, and abandonment to the dance that comes from believing in God and the resurrection.' When I look at the historical Jesus, I think what a wonderful man he was. I know that inside myself I want to be like him, as fully and completely human as I can be, integrated and whole within.

That desire sits four square within the challenges that

the Gospel gives us. We are invited to constantly reflect on what it means to be a human being and to be open enough to really discover what that means. It is an invitation to own our inner life and all the energies and emotions that are within us. It is an invitation to know the abiding embrace of God in the midst of a humanity that is sacred and holy. It is an invitation to be in relationship with ourselves, the world, with God, and with humanity. To become a person who understands what humanity is about, who loves the gift of life and who enters into it, is to witness to the reality of the Gospel in a way that brings life ourselves and to others.

We all want to be human and alive. That desire has been planted in our hearts by God. Look deeply within yourself. Learn to embrace what you find. Begin the process of letting go of what you have to let go of and you will then begin to understand and really value your own humanity. In the book of Deuteronomy we hear the author say to us, choose life. As we move towards wholeness and integration we will experience a rich deep inner life. So do not be afraid of your inner condition. Love yourself with all your imperfections and you may just discover that they in fact are your greatest gift.

NINE

THE EXODUS JOURNEY

I am forever meeting people who have extraordinary stories to tell. One of them was a man called Phil who turned up at our community meeting one night and stayed for several years. He was an interesting man in his mid thirties. As I got to know him he shared more and more of his story, a story that had led him to travel the world looking for fulfilment.

He said that he tired of sex, drugs, and rock and roll very quickly. When he found that those things did not satisfy he went off to India. He travelled around the country taking some solace in meditation and in the discovery of some of the ancient Religions but still it was not enough. He left India and wandered around Europe for many years. His journey seemed never ending and his quest for peace seemed destined not to be fulfilled. At some point Phil had an encounter with Christianity, that awoke within him his latent Catholicism, and he felt he wanted to pursue his search. Christianity and the person of Jesus fascinated him and seemed to meet some of the ache within. He came back to Southport where he had lived as a child and found our community.

I remember thinking at the time that his journey had been an epic journey from darkness to light, slavery to freedom and it reminded me of the ancient story of the exodus. There had been much slavery and at times darkness in Phil's life. He had wandered in the desert trying to find God until eventually he found the promised land in the presence of Christ.

The exodus is probably the central truth of the First Testament. It's an image of the journey that every person makes when he or she sets out to find God. Very simply the word Israel means people of God. The people in the First Testament story of the Exodus represent the whole of humanity and what happened to them happens to us when we set out on that epic journey of discovery of ourselves and God.

In the book of Exodus, Egypt is the place of slavery and the Promised Land the place of freedom. We enter the Promised Land when we discover freedom within ourselves. It is the place that all people of faith have to journey towards. It seems to me that the only way in which we will recognise the importance of unity at every level is when it happens within us.

Over the last fifteen years I have worked with many groups and one of the areas that we always touch on is the inner life and the way in which we have to work on what happens inside us to find life. It is another way of expressing this exodus journey that we all have to make. It is the way in which we work on our inner reality to reach the Promised Land. It is all about spirituality. I guess at some level we human beings need to do a lot of work on our inner life if we are not to be stunted in our growth and to become more a force for disunity than unity.

This exodus journey towards the Promised Land is all about what Richard Rohr calls soul work. It is about the willingness to go deep within ourselves and discover the reality that gives life, whilst dealing with all the fragmentation and brokenness that we find on the way. A couple of years ago I was on the ferry from Ireland to Liverpool and got into conversation with an Irish man. He asked me what I did and I told him I was involved in spirituality and he asked me to give him a working man's definition. Before I could speak, the person who was with me said it is about a thirst for life.

It seems as though the more we journey into who we are and face who we are, the more able we are to let go of the dross that stops us experiencing the real life that we all thirst for. The more we let go, the more room we are able to give to God and the more room we give God, the more we discover what it means to be human and alive. The fullness of humanity is, of course, only found in true intimacy with God. It is then that we will recognise the invitation to be united within ourselves, with God, with our brothers and sisters and with the world. In many senses that has to be the promised land.

When we begin to work on our inner lives, the way in which we live externally changes. The things that are important to us change. The values that matter to us change. Our lives begin to take on order and purpose. We behave differently at work, at home, with our friends.

A few years ago I was invited to work with a group of women. This group was founded nearly forty years ago and it provides a place for women to come together and share what is going on inside them. They were very strong, free people who knew who they were and who experienced a great degree of wholeness because of the time they spend reflecting. They discovered that what went on within them had a great deal to do with what goes on outside them. They were a wonderful group of human beings because they were rooted and grounded in a deep inner life, which was what had slaked their thirst and enabled them to explore themselves and the world.

They were involved in all sorts of things to do with the environment. They were into Ignatian spirituality.

Several of them were trained Spiritual Directors. There were psychotherapists and counsellors. Many of them seemed to have found what it was that would answer their thirst for life. What they were finding on the inside affected the outside. What amazed me was that what they were doing was creating unity, mirroring the creative force at the heart of the universe.

The journey told in the book of Exodus, from the place of slavery to the Promised Land, is an epic tale which symbolises our own struggle from slavery to freedom. The experience of Israel is the same experience we are called into, as God liberates us and slakes our thirst for life. I suppose one of the questions to ask ourselves today is what is our Egypt? What is it that causes fragmentation within? Where are we held in slavery deep within? Are we slaves to money? So many people think what they have is the key to life. Are we slaves to sex? Is that what we think will help us live life to the full? What about power? Do we build our own little kingdoms where we are in charge and in control to make ourselves feel good about ourselves? It is amazing how often Jesus in the Gospels talks about power.

Are we slaves to religion, running around after this visionary or that one, taking refuge in ritual and legalism? It is amazing how often Jesus condemned the Religious people of his day. Are we slaves to fear?

And how, as people of faith, do we react to our slavery? You see until we look at Exodus as a symbolic story of religious truth, something that we all have to go through, much of what we read seems a long way removed from our experience. It is hard to believe the things that we read and, if we take it all literally, then the temptation is to say that God worked wonders then but not any more.

The original Exodus experience happened somewhere between 2000 and 1200 BC. The Scripture scholars tell us that it is very likely that those who escaped were a group of individuals who were enslaved together. What made them a people and gave them an identity was the experience of Exodus. The key man in the story is Moses. He led the people out of Egypt. Moses, who had to make the journey within himself before he could lead others out.

His story begins when his mother, in order to save his life, puts him in a basket on the Nile. The Pharaoh's daughter found the basket and as she looks in it, a young girl darts out of the reeds nearby and says that she knows a Hebrew woman who could suckle the child for her. The little girl is Miriam, Moses' sister, and the woman his natural mother. So Moses grows up knowing that he is a Hebrew despite being brought up by an Egyptian princess.

It is hard to live in two worlds and yet many of us do it. We have our holy world and our secular world and we are not the same in both. It is fragmentation, it is about being disunited with oneself. That is what it was like for Moses. He had a sense of being a Hebrew yet he lived in the world of the Egyptians. We have an innate sense of God calling us to go deep within and discover the values that make the kingdom real, that unites us within and without, but our vision is clouded by the materialism and cynicism of the world all around us.

Most of us give in and the forces that drive the world govern our lives, power, prestige, possessions, the need to succeed. Faith gives way to market forces. The question we all have to ask is, which world are we going to live in? The world in which the values of unity are of paramount importance, reconciliation, inner stability, forgiveness, love, and compassion. Or will power, prestige, possessions, the need to succeed, all of which cause more and more disintegration and individualism, rule our lives?

Moses made his choice. One day he saw an Egyptian slave driver beating a Hebrew and he was so angry that he killed the slave driver and then ran away frightened of what Pharaoh might do. It is from that place of fear that Moses begins his journey in faith. He hides away working as a shepherd.

Fear is an interesting reality. Most of us operate a lot of the time from fear and it blocks us becoming the people God created us to be. Moses was not meant to be a shepherd. It was his fear that kept him there. I have said on many occasions that it is fundamental to the Scriptural message that we do not need to be afraid. Yet so many of us live bound up by fear and it keeps us from journeying towards the Promised Land. It keeps us from believing in the truth of God's presence. It causes disunity and isolation. When I was ill with depression, one of my biggest fears was not being the successful Priest, so I cut myself off from others.

We have been fed the success ethic so much that the fear of not living up to what we think we should be can cripple us. So many of us are frightened of our emotional lives. I have been working recently with a policeman who is so afraid of the anger that lies within him, so afraid that it will burst out and do some real damage. I know there are times in my life when anger bubbles just below the surface it frightens me. Why are we so afraid of our emotions? Why is it that we do not face pain very well and run away from it? Why do we opt out of many situations that make us face up to that pain? Our emotions have to be faced and worked through if we are going to find life, otherwise they burst out inappropriately in anger or in action that does nothing to build up the kingdom of unity and peace.

We are afraid of what others will think so we do not rock the boat or say anything controversial. We become real systems people trusting all the time in whatever system we have invested ourselves in, social, political or Religious. Trusting more in the system rather than in God. Many people are afraid that society is crashing down around our ears, afraid for our children and our futures. I love the words of Julian of Norwich: 'All will be well. All manner of things will be well.' We do not trust it.'

As a nation we seem to be frightened of the asylum seekers and refugees. They make us feel afraid. They are different. They have another culture and it threatens us. We can see what fear is doing to the nations as one nation wars against another and protects itself at all costs from the other. We no sooner recover from one war than we are threatened with the next. We are so afraid of one another.

The greatest enemy of being people of faith is fear. It keeps so many people from that deep listening and that deep trusting in the God who is present, as we journey within. Fear is what keeps us from being united with others. The invitation is to face that fear within and work through it so that we can become what God wants us to become.

The story of the burning bush is a lovely story because it shows how reluctant Moses is to do what God wants. His fears have almost submerged him. This man of faith is going to be dragged screaming and shouting. He is not going to give up his quiet way of life easily. He is not going to face his fears without a struggle.

People of faith in the Scriptures are never plaster saints any more than we are. They are usually people who have to work through their worries and fears and face their sinfulness. They are usually people who make mistakes but who spend the time reflecting and learning from their lives. Often they are people who do not want to do what they are called to do but who go anyway, aware that it is the only way.

I do not know why we get the idea that people of faith are these mealy-mouthed people that we often see in our churches, who equate faith with being good, and are usually very boring. People of faith are those who live life with all its ups and downs and discover the presence of God in it all. People of faith are those who are open to otherness and who are not afraid of themselves, the world or other people.

So Moses was not one of those people who look as though they are sucking a gooseberry. He met a God of power in the story of the burning bush in Exodus 3.

He had to face his fears and what he had done. He had to cope with the murder that he had committed and he had to learn to trust. That experience changed his life and gave him purpose and direction as he was called to tell Pharaoh, 'Let my people go.'

In Moses' story we see a pattern, which is repeated often in the Scriptures. One person listens to the Lord and that person is used to lead the people forward in their journey of faith. One of the interesting aspects of Moses' story is that God does not tell him how to lead the people out he simply says trust me. It is a major theme in the First Testament.

Moses is willing to take the risk to trust God and to go on the journey. I do not know about you but I sometimes think we have forgotten about the risk element in following the Lord. We have made faith about prayer, about contemplation, about liturgy and about knowledge. Biblical faith is about risk and relationship and never knowing, just trusting.

Unless you have fallen in love with God you will not be prepared to risk. You will have too much to protect: your reputation, your status, your part in the system. If you have fallen in love with God none of that will really matter. You will hold it all very lightly. But in order for that transformation to take place we have to work on the inner life.

We then have a contrast between Moses and the people he calls and I guess many of us will see our faith journey more in the people he calls than in Moses' story himself. He tells the people that he believes in the promise of God to set his people free and after a struggle they eventually believe him and begin to believe that there is nothing that can stop what God has promised happening. In many ways it is like our response to the Good News of God's love.

There is a struggle to accept it. When we do manage to do that, to some degree, there is a surge within of belief that, with God, all our problems are over. Nothing can get in the way; but the truth is, it can and it does. We see that happening in the hardness of Pharaoh and the securities of the system. Pharaoh refuses to listen to Moses and to Aaron his brother and accuses them of luring the Israelites from their work, so he doubles the work of the Israelites, who soon begin to doubt Moses and groan about their plight. They want nothing else to do with God. There is a constant battle in this story between unity and disunity.

Humanity never seems to learn from the lessons of history and so the Exodus story is not too far removed from the way we are. As soon as things get difficult we turn away, not prepared to walk the journey, not prepared to trust the promise. Moses stands as a challenge to us all, not to give up in this journey of faith but to keep on going. We are to keep on facing our fears, keep on dealing with our anger and our bitterness, keep on inviting God to deliver us from our 'Egypts', whatever they may be, so that we can live life to the full in perfect unity.

What we discover is that God is faithful, faithful to Moses on his journey in faith and faithful to the people on theirs. I am quite sure at the time it was all happening the Israelites did not recognise what God was doing but in hindsight they did and so they wrote down the action of God's saving power. I am sure the same is true for us. It is only in hindsight that we recognise what God is doing in our lives and how his love is constantly liberating us and setting us free and drawing us together within, as well as with others and with God.

When we are actually in the experience we do not always see that God is at work. In fact, usually we cannot see God at work at all, we simply have to trust. Faith is not about certitude. It is about feeling the way and believing in the promise of God. That is the challenge that was given to the Israelites. We discover in the book of Exodus that they spent 40 years in the Sinai desert. They went round in circles and seemed to be going nowhere. Someone once said to me that the journey should only have taken them eleven days.

Every time the people found an oasis in the desert, they wanted to stay there and when Moses moved them on and reminded them of the Lord's promise, they would hark back to Egypt and say they were better off there. Have you ever done that when the going gets tough wished you had never started out? Have you ever stayed in your own Egypt because the risk is too great to move on?

You see, the people of Israel are really no different to us, because the temptation for any of us who start out on the journey of faith, is to turn back. The journey will lead us to be like Moses, challenging people because we live unafraid of others. Having faced our own fears others hold no fear for us. The journey will challenge others because we will have let go of the need to succeed. The journey will lead us to challenge people by our lifestyle, through our willingness to forgive and stand with one another and with those who are different to us.

It will bring us face to face with injustice and bigotry and when we have to make a stand in the face of opposition, we might find ourselves saying, 'I wish I did not have to do this. It was easier before. It was easier when I did not forgive. It was easier when I did not notice people starving. It was easier when I did not understand that I was a part of something bigger than myself. It was easier to be religious than to be a person of faith.'

I am discovering more and more that there is a huge difference between being people of faith and people who are religious. Religion offers its own security. It can make us feel safe. It can make us feel right and certain. It can make us self-satisfied and self-righteous. It can be so easy to stay locked into the narrow confines of religion and make them our security and never become what God is calling us to be. We never become people who are open to journey and discovery. We do not have to become people who are willing to let go of what we thought we knew so that God can lead us a little further into truth. We become people who are always dividing and separating because of our need to be right at another's expense.

The Challenge is always to be a person of faith, to grow in trust day by day. That is the essential lesson of the desert. When the Lord sends them manna from the desert, he tells Moses to tell the people only to pick up enough food for themselves for the day. What is it saying? 'Trust me'. That lesson always goes against the grain because we always want to plan for the future but the lesson is to let go, give up control and surrender to the Lord. As human beings we are not very good at that. We want to be in control and plan things out but that is not the way of faith.

As the people of Israel stepped out into the desert they did it on the crest of a wave but instead of getting stronger as they went along, they experienced weakness and weariness. There was division amongst them. They obviously were not as strong as they thought they were. The same thing often happens to us.

When our securities, our defence mechanisms, our safe explanations, are taken away from us we find out who we really are. Even when those securities are things like bitterness, lack of forgiveness, or hatred, their absence makes us question and what we discover is how small we are and the only place to go is to the one who re-creates us. It is then that we will learn the lesson of the desert.

The sadness is that all too often we do not learn the lesson. We do not face our emotions and work them through. We blame and accuse rather than process what is going on inside us and of course that leads to separation rather than unity. In its worst extremes wars and battles and destruction occur.

After the Hebrews go through the Red Sea the writer of the book says this in chapter 14:31: 'the people put their faith in Yahweh and in his servant Moses.' Trust in God goes hand in hand with trust in other people. It is not just God and me. Faith in God and faith in people work together and form community. If we become human beings of faith we are to form community. It is unity all the way. So the Israelites set out into the desert again and the author of the book says that Yahweh was with them, a pillar of fire by night and a pillar of cloud by day. None of the people knew where they were going. They had to trust in God and in God's timing. When the pillar stopped they had to stop and they did not move forward until God led them forward. The lesson of trust and responding to God's timing is a long and difficult one to learn but if we're to experience the Promised Land we have to make the journey.

The Book of Exodus ends with God still leading the people forward into history. It is interesting that Moses never entered the Promised Land, but maybe he did not have to because he was already experiencing it. He was walking the journey of faith, living in the Kingdom. He had met the Lord and so did not have to go anywhere else to meet him. His life had been given for unity. His journey was over before it ended. In a sense God gave him the Promised Land before he got there. It can be like that for us if we learn the lessons the Scriptures teach us of facing ourselves and trusting and surrendering.

Our experience is more likely to be that of the people of Israel wandering round in circles in the desert, trying to learn the lesson of trust but always doubting and fearing. 'Will God really be God?' In spite of those doubts and fears the Lord's promise will still be the same as it was to Israel and the same as it was to Moses. Surrender, learn to trust and God will give you life, unity, and deep peace.

TEN

BETTER TOGETHER

Many years ago I got to know a community in Liverpool. They lived in what was a very tough area but the members of that community felt that they had been called there by God. What was interesting and very challenging was the make up of that community. It consisted of two nuns from different orders, one a semi-contemplative. There was a retired Catholic Priest and then two families, who were from a Free Church background.

They went to the local council and asked for somewhere to live and eventually settled in a small block of flats which they bought from the council and worked on to make them habitable. They lived together in peace and harmony knowing that there was more uniting them than could ever divide them.

Their presence in the town had a major effect on the local community. At first people in the area just saw them as 'do gooders', who would eventually get fed up and move away, after all people had moved in before 'sent by God'. When that move did not happen people began to ask the question 'why would they be here in this place with us?' Eventually that small community drew around them a praying group of people who still meet today. People began to move into the area who had a pride in the place in which they lived. That had a knock-on effect as residents who had given up hope began to take a pride in their environment.

As the community grew they began to make links with all sorts of people around their town, particularly young people that everyone else had given up on. I remember being with them one night, praying, when the roof of the room we were in collapsed and a body fell into our midst. Of course people screamed and then we heard the laughter on the roof. The local gang leaders had chipped away until the ceiling collapsed and dropped a scarecrow into our midst as a warning. Once the furore had died down, the prayer continued. Some of those same gang leaders in time became part of that community.

As the years have gone by, the priest has died, the sisters have been recalled to their own religious orders and one of the founding couples has died but that community remains. There have been crisis times but they have remained faithful. They are vibrant, lively and inter-denominational. Simply being together has had a profound impact where they live and further afield. Unity makes a difference.

All Christians hold the basic truth in common that 'God so loved the world'. That same God, the immense creative force that holds everything in being, became a human being to show us the depth of creative love. The Word became flesh. Yet for centuries we lived deeply suspicious of people who were not of our faith tradition.

As Catholics we did not read the Scriptures personally, because that is what 'the Protestants' did. My mum used to tell me of the time when it was forbidden to pray in a Church that was not of one's own tradition. It was extraordinarily difficult to get married to a person who had a different belief system. I have heard horror stories of people having to become Catholics in order to get married in Church and others rejected by their own families for marrying someone not of their own tradition.

We may think we live in more enlightened times but do we really? Is there still not evidence of bigotry and suspicion amongst Christian traditions and between world faiths?

Ronald Rolheiser the Canadian oblate and spiritual author, who I quote often says, 'At a time when misunderstanding, anger, intolerance, impatience, lack of respect, and lack of charity are paralysing our communities and dividing the sincere from the sincere, it is time for us, followers of Jesus called to imitate his wide compassion, to re-ground ourselves in some fundamentals: respect, charity, understanding, patience, and gentleness towards those who oppose us. It is time to accept, too, that we are all in this together, one family within which everyone needs everyone else. There is no 'we' and 'them', there's only 'us'.

As I have already shared, when I was 15 my faith came to life. God found me and helped me to understand my own dignity and value. As a Catholic I started going back to Mass. I had not realised at that time there were any barriers between Christians of different denominations and so in 1975 I used to go quite happily to a small Anglican Church to pray with people there. I used to go along to the community that I have just written about and was welcomed and accepted. We gathered knowing that Christ was with us and, yes, we might use different words and have slightly different understandings but Christ was present and it was not about 'us' and 'them'. As Rolheiser says there was no differential, only us and the Lord was present.

I think Rolheiser's understanding was at the heart of the Second Vatican Council's teaching on ecumenism and inter-faith relationships. With the advent of the Second Vatican Council and the decree on ecumenism there was an acknowledgment of blame on all sides for the controversies underlying divisions among Christians. The document on ecumenism said that Catholics should seek dialogue and unity with 'our separated brethren.' Then in the document called 'the declaration on religious liberty' it was argued that the basic dignity of human beings demands freedom from coercion in matters of religion. All people should be free to worship according to their own conscience.

The Council did something extraordinary when, in those forward-looking documents on ecumenism and non-Christian religions, it makes clear that there are some constant themes, truths, and recurrences, in all of the world religions.

To quote the document on non-Christian religions the Council fathers say, 'All peoples comprise a single community and have a single origin [created by one and the same Creator God]... And one also is their final goal: God... The Catholic Church rejects nothing which is true and holy in these religions.'

Then the document goes on to praise Native religions, Hinduism, Judaism, Buddhism, and Islam as 'reflecting a ray of that truth which enlightens all people.' To think that was written in the early 1960's and yet most Catholics today are still deeply suspicious of other Christian traditions let alone other world faiths. I know good people who will denounce Buddhism and Hinduism as being of the devil. That is not Catholic teaching. Have we really explored what it means to be a child of the Second Vatican Council? I think not.

For most people within the Catholic tradition, Vatican II was merely a change in the liturgy, when in fact, it was a challenging and deep call to dialogue and unity that many Catholics have never realised and probably never really wanted. It is far easier to stay in the self righteous place of being right than to enter into dialogue and mutual respect.

Derek Worlock, who was a former Archbishop of Liverpool, was well known for his desire for unity. As a young man he had been an observer at the Council and said this: 'The Second Vatican Council was a powerful call for renewal spiritually, liturgically, socially, and politically. It was the occasion for new insights and understanding of the nature of the church, of shared responsibility, of true relationships between distinct ministries, of equality of dignity of all in the sight of God, and of the need to reach out with the good news of the Gospel towards those bewildered or misled in a self-centred world.' Note the powerful call to renewal. Note the reminder of the dignity of all in the sight of God. It was all about unity within the Church and beyond.

All the Popes since the second Vatican Council have picked up that call to unity primarily between Christians but always aware of the goodness that lies in other faiths too.

Paul V1 who re-convened the Second Vatican Council on the death of John twenty third met on several occasions with the leaders of other traditions and published a united statement with the Anglican Church in 1966.

Pope and now Saint John Paul II said in his document *Et Unum Sint*, 'Thus it is absolutely clear that ecumenism, the movement promoting Christian unity, is not just some sort of 'appendix' which is added to the Church's traditional activity. Rather, ecumenism is an organic part of her life and work, and consequently must pervade all that she is and does.'

How many of us are willing to explore what Christian unity might be about? In one of our local villages the Christian churches do as much together as they possibly can. Each Good Friday they hold a Passion play with a visiting speaker which brings the village centre to a halt. There are four or five hundred people walking there, united in faith. What is interesting is that it is the Catholics in the village who are the prime movers in gathering and sustaining the presence of the Church in village life. I think those people recognise the call of Vatican II to be united with others of faith but it is not a picture that is replicated widely in the areas I know.

Just a little further on in a town with several Catholic churches there is an ecumenical gathering each week. The Catholics, sadly, are the least well represented. That picture I would say is far more common.

Benedict XV1 said very powerfully at the celebration of vespers for the week of Christian unity in 2013, 'Full and visible communion among Christians is to be understood, in fact, as a fundamental characteristic for an ever clearer witness. As we journey towards full unity, it is thus necessary to pursue a practical collaboration among the disciples of Christ for the cause of transmitting the faith to the contemporary world. Today there is great need for reconciliation, dialogue and mutual understanding — not in a moralistic perspective but as authentic Christians for an ever stronger presence in the context of our time.'

Pope Francis is extraordinarily keen to promote unity. He has welcomed to the Vatican both formally and informally people of other traditions and other faiths. He has recently encouraged those of us in the Catholic tradition to open ourselves to others who share our journey when he said, 'In my many encounters or correspondence with other Christians, I see a strong desire to walk and pray together, to know and love the Lord and to work together in the service of the weak and suffering. On this common journey, I am convinced that, under the guidance of the Holy Spirit, we can learn from each other and grow into the communion which already unites us.'

In 2014 he said this: 'Unity does not imply uniformity; it does not necessarily mean doing everything together or thinking in the same way. Nor does it signify a loss of identity. Unity in diversity is actually the opposite: it involves the joyful recognition and acceptance of the various gifts which the Holy Spirit gives to each one and the placing of these gifts at the service of all members of the Church. It means knowing how to listen, to accept differences, and having the freedom to think differently and express oneself with complete respect towards the other, who is my brother or sister. Do not be afraid of differences!'

Often it is the fear of otherness that keep us apart from one another. It is the refusal to listen and accept otherness that might challenge deeply held beliefs. It is the need to be right which necessitates someone else to be wrong. It is the unwillingness to recognise that we share a common humanity that unites us. I have written before of Jay, a Hindu by birth, who became one of my

closest friends. We would share much in common and
lovingly accept our differences. I remember when I was
a University Chaplain I met a young atheistic Jew
called David. He would come along to our journey in
faith group and shared and discussed and sat
respectfully when we prayed. He made many people
think, but the group was stronger and more rooted
because of him. There is no need to be afraid of
otherness and difference.

Cardinal Cormac Murphy O'Connor when addressing
the Anglican synod in Chichester in 1978 said this, 'We
Christians are meant to be the light and the hope of
the world, because we claim to live our lives in union
with Christ, Emmanuel, which means, 'God with us'.
We are here to witness to the world the deeper things
which give life and vision, which bring joy and hope to
our society. But the fact is that we should somehow do
this together, not just for our own sake but for the sake
of people who need the vision and hope and trust that
are in Jesus Christ.'

It is by being together that we give the fullest expression
of the body of Christ and reveal the presence of Christ
to the world. One of our community is involved in a
Soup Kitchen which has volunteers from many
different churches and none. The co-operation and the
harmony that exists between them as they look after

and care for the most broken in society really is the best witness to Christ that there could possibly be.

That is why Cardinal Cormac went on to say in his address, 'The primary purpose of ecumenism is not just for churches to come together, but rather that together they may give witness to Christ. 'May they all be one, Father, may they be one in us, as you are in me and I am in you, so that the world may believe it was you who sent me' (John 17:21). But how much do we care?

How important it is to remember that, in the area of ecumenism, it is no longer the object to convert the other to one's own private view; the purpose of our meeting each other is not that the other turn from his wrong or wicked ways, but that each one of us should; the conversion we demand is our own, and that is painful. 'There can be no ecumenism worthy of the name without interior conversion, for it is from newness of attitudes of mind, from self-denial and unstinted love, that desires of unity take their rise and develop in a mature way'

It is incredibly challenging to realise that to be ecumenical demands a deep conversion within us. It invites us to let go, which is never easy. Several years ago I was invited to go and speak at a local Pentecostal church. When I arrived I followed people into the main hall without announcing who I was. I was a stranger and the people there made me feel very welcome. I was assigned to Edna and her friend Marie who would 'look after me for the evening' I was told. I still had not told them that I was the main speaker that night.

As we sat with our cup of tea these two lovely women began to share with me some of their fears for that evening. They began to tell me that it was the first time that a Catholic had been invited to speak at this Church. They questioned the wisdom of their pastor in asking a Priest to come. They began to talk about the Catholic Church in less than helpful ways. They talked of worshipping Mary and the Saints and questioned the authority structure of the Church. As I was about to tell them who I was, the pastor who had invited me, came into the room, spied me and came over. He swept me away telling these two ladies that I was the speaker for the evening and leaving them looking and, I guess, feeling, incredibly sheepish.

That night I spoke about my own faith journey and at the end prayed with the people. When the meeting was finished Edna and Marie came across to me. They very lovingly and humbly apologised and said that I had made them think completely differently about Catholics. They apologised for their intransigence and ill-informed opinion. When I left the Church I was filled with respect for those two women who had allowed the spirit to change their attitudes that night.

As I think about Kirkby and that small Anglican prayer group, and also reflect on the teaching of the Church, I have realised that what was happening at a grass roots level in my own life and the lives of countless others was being echoed in the higher eschalons of the Church. Unity and the quest for it is of vital importance and core to what the Church is about. You see, the spirit was and is doing something incredible in and amongst the churches. This spirit knows no boundaries as the power of God cuts through centuries of mistrust and suspicion and enables us to stretch out our hands to others from different traditions and celebrate the truth that we are all children of God.

I think that after the Vatican Council there was a spirit of hope and enthusiasm amongst the Church traditions that had never been felt before as we began to try to journey together. It was not a negating of one's own tradition, as some thought. It was an awareness of what the spirit was doing across the churches and a moving with that spirit.

Why would God's spirit work in that way? Why sweep away the years of mistrust and break down barriers that had divided God's people? I think because it was only

thing that God could do! In the heart of God there is
no room for separation or division. As I said in the first
chapter of this book, God is perfect unity and we as
individuals and community are made in the image and
likeness of God. We cannot show the face of God to the
world when we are divided.

I guess that is why I think we need to hear again the
call to unity, to come together and do as much as we
possibly can together. I think we are being invited by
God to challenge anything that would uphold disunity
between different traditions and to stand against the
scandal of disunity.

Sadly after the initial response to the Vatican Council
and its call to unity, many people have lost heart. Will
it ever happen? Are we just wasting our time? I do not
think we are. We can never let suspicion and fear rear
its ugly head again. We must never allow struggles for
power, jockeying for position, and wanting our own way
to destroy the simple call to be united in love. Our need
to be right and orthodox has to be given up in order to
journey and discover. How can we create camps of the
like-minded that become exclusive rather than inclusive
when all the time that fails to show the face of God to
the world.

The greatest witness we have today is unity. It is what

will convince the world of the presence of God. Moralising or making dogmatic statements will never do it; only people who come together in love, to share love with one another and the world. What will convince the world of the reality of God are groups of people who know how to stand with those in need; people who know how to celebrate love and life together.

I was invited some years ago to speak at a camp which takes place every year in North Yorkshire. What I found most moving, and challenging for some, was that those who gathered at the camp were of a variety of persuasions, Catholics, Pentecostals, High Anglicans, and others from a house church background. There were young people and old people and children. What I found most moving was that there were also people there who struggled with their sexuality. There were people who were in broken and damaged relationships and there were some who had experienced rejection and alienation from main-line churches. Yet in that place was a love and a unity that I have never experienced before. It is that unity that is a witness to the reality of the Gospel. It is not comfortable or easy but it is life giving.

To live a fully Christian life is to give your life for unity. To simply accept disunity and not seek to overcome it is a scandal. I know that the Church is a human institution and, some would say, therefore bound to fail. I think I would want to say that the Church is also a sacrament; yes, made up of broken frail human beings but it is a reality that has been created by God. As Jesus can be described as the Sacrament or sign of God so can the Church be considered as both a sign of and reality of the Risen Christ.

In other words we are to be a meaningful sign to all people, believers and non-believers. It is a sacrament because it is the Body of Christ. It is his continuing presence at work in the world. He is present wherever there is love, forgiveness, mercy, kindness, and healing. He is there wherever the poor and broken are being cared for. How much more effective is that witness when we are united. So, seen from God's perspective, all disunity and self-seeking is a scandal because it reduces the effectiveness of that body. The present Archbishop of Canterbury, Justin Welby, described it more strongly as an 'obscenity'.

I remember feeling deeply ashamed at an open ecumenical meeting a long time ago. What can only be described as a row broke out between a vociferous Catholic woman and a man who was a High Anglican. The row was about what the woman called transubstantiation. The man had simply said that he did not understand the word. The woman was furious and had not really heard what was said. She thought that he was denying Christ's presence in the Eucharist. So she was, as far as she was concerned, defending her Catholic faith. When the man said that he, too, believed that Christ was present, body, blood, soul and divinity in the Eucharist she said that he could not possibly believe that because he was a Protestant. She actually used a far more derogatory term than that. It was then that another man stood up and said that he had come to the meeting out of interest. He wanted to see how close the churches were becoming. He said that all he felt was sadness as people confirmed his decision to have nothing to do with church because there was no love there. He then left the room having reduced it to silence. I felt deeply saddened that our disunity had that effect on him but I think, had I not been so invested in Church and all it means, that I might have followed him. It is indeed an obscenity to promulgate disunity.

So we are called to give our lives for the unity of the Church, the world, and all of humanity. To do that will turn our lives upside down. It will change our image of God and where God can be found. It will challenge us deeply within as we have to let go of our need to be right and others to be wrong. It will call us into relationship with others who see things differently or whose journey has led them on a different path than the one we have trodden.

But it will bring us life as we enter into the immense
work of God and show the face of God to the world.
I love the film 'Dead Poets Society' starring the
wonderful, yet tortured, Robin Williams, and its mantra
'Seize the day'. I think we are to do just that in our
quest for unity. Seize the day, begin now, because now
is all we have.

ELEVEN

THE EUCHARIST
CALLS US TO UNITY

It was a dark cold January evening. We had just finished serving the last of our visitors when the door bell rang again. When I opened the door it was Simon. He was a man in his thirties who had learning difficulties and a very bad stammer who had come to our town to look for seasonal work. He had managed to find himself a damp bed sit so was not technically homeless but Simon lived way below the poverty line. Eventually someone told him that there might be food and help available at the Church. So Simon had come to us for food when he lost his job. Social services paid his rent but he had little else.

It took a great deal of coaxing and time to get Simon to trust us. At first he hardly spoke, took what we gave him and left. Eventually, as time went on, we discovered that he had been badly bullied in the North East pit village that he came from and that he had a mother and a sister still living in that place. His mum was housebound and his sister looked after her. They had been instrumental in his leaving. Simon had eventually had enough of the bullies and the taunts. He had lost his temper and ended up in court. He just avoided a custodial sentence. Simon's mum and sister both knew that without a fresh start Simon was heading for prison. So they managed to get some money together, put him on a bus and he had ended up in Southport looking for seasonal work.

Every Saturday night when he thought everyone else had left he would knock on the door. Haltingly and with a great deal of effort he would ask for his needs and we would try and help. After about eighteen months, when we discovered that he had family, I suggested that he might like to ring and speak to his mum. For a variety of reasons, not least his communication difficulties, he had not spoken to her since the day he left. I remember the first day that he phoned her. He asked me to stay with him in case his mum could not understand him. Simon started to cry when he heard her voice and when he said, 'I love you mum', I had a sense of the presence of God in the very real love between the two of them and it took my breath away. It was one of those Gospel moments when I knew that God was present.

I have a sneaking suspicion that the end of John's Gospel is all about presence and how we recognise the presence of the risen Jesus. Where do we find this Lord? One of the truths of John's Gospel is that we find the spiritual through the material.

If the incarnation means anything at all, it means that God has chosen to be with us not in some vague other-worldly sense but in the material of this world and so everything is sacred for eyes that can see. Everything. I have often quoted the words of the poet Elizabeth Barrett Browning when she wrote, 'Every bush is alive with the glory of God but only those who see take off their shoes, the rest sit and eat blackberries.' We seem so blind to the presence of God in our midst. Maybe it is because we focus too much on the 'blackberries'.

I often think that the biggest change in us that has to take place is in the realm of awareness, of becoming aware of the God who is in all things and who is constantly trying to communicate with us. To become aware of the presence of the risen Jesus in our midst in every person that we look at, in every breath we take.

There is a sense in which our cry has to be that of the blind man from chapter 9 of John's Gospel, 'Lord that I may see'. It is an invitation to God to set us free from our false perceptions and dualistic mentality, as well as the attitudes of heart and mind that blind us to God's presence so that we may see.

Jean Vanier says in his book *Drawn into the Mystery of Jesus*: 'The conclusion of the gospel of John is very gentle. We are back in Galilee, the home of Jesus and his disciples. All the surprising, exciting, wonderful, stimulating, and tragic events are over. We are in the ordinariness of simple daily life.'

In the final resurrection appearance John is trying to tell his community and through them, us, that it is in the ordinariness of life that we will find this risen Jesus, if we only have eyes to look. People of faith are invited to see that this risen Lord is everywhere even and perhaps primarily in the day-to-day grind of daily life.

As a part-time prison chaplain while training to be a Priest, I met many people whose lives had taken them to the bottom of the pile. It was often our job to pick up the pieces when marriages or long term relationships had broken down under the strain of imprisonment. We were the ones called in to break bad news or to spend time with someone who had received bad news. It was a steep learning curve for someone like me in their mid-twenties.

I remember very clearly having to go and see Peter. His mother had died and he had attempted suicide shortly after he was told. He was in the hospital wing and he wanted to see the chaplain. It was one of my evenings on duty and so I went across to see him. He was a sad broken man, who wept as he shared with me how much he loved his mum. It seemed that she was the only stable influence in his life and now she, too, was gone.

As I listened to him and tried to help him, a strange thing happened. A mental image of Robert Powell filled my mind. I saw him as Christ in the Franco Zefferelli production of Jesus of Nazareth. I do not claim a vision because what I saw in my mind was a famous image with the crown of thorns on his head, pushed down into his skull and the blood running down his cheeks. What I do believe is that in that moment I had a revelation of the suffering Christ in Peter as he wept and shared his pain. I realised that I was sitting before Christ; that he was as real to me in this man, Peter, as he would have been had I been at Calvary. It took my breath away and I wept with him. Later he said to me that it was only when I cried that he realised that I understood. It is in the ordinary experiences of life that we recognise Christ. In fact his passion, death and resurrection is going on in our lives constantly.

So what is happening at the end of John's Gospel? After the dramatic death and claims of resurrection, Peter and the others have gone back to what they were sure of, back to fishing. They are not sure of anything else, so they went out and got into the boat to fish and caught nothing.

They were on the way back and saw a stranger on the

shore who called out to them asking if had they caught anything. In response to their answer, 'No', the stranger invites them to cast their net again. You can imagine them looking at one another and wondering what was happening. It was only when Jesus spoke that they caught anything. It says something powerful about the word of God and the invitation to reflect on it, to make it the bed-rock of our lives. It is only the word of God that will bear fruit in our lives.

The disciples are in a boat, they see the stranger on the shore and the beloved disciple is able to recognise Jesus. If you and I love, then we will recognise the presence of Jesus and know it is the Lord when he speaks. So John says, 'It is the Lord.' When Peter and the others arrive at the shore we find a charcoal fire waiting. Jesus gives them some bread and cooks the fish and shares it with them.

It is a meal that symbolises every other meal that has taken place in John's Gospel, the wedding feast at Cana, the multiplication of the loaves and the fish in chapter six and the reflection after it, the meals that took place with those who followed the Lord like Martha and Mary in chapter twelve. The last meal with the disciples in chapter thirteen. They are all there, captured in some bread and some fish, on the sea shore. 'Come and have breakfast. Come and eat.' We are told that none of them dared ask who he was. They knew it was the Lord. They all recognised him.

I think the author of the Gospel is inviting us to recognise the presence of the Lord in our Eucharistic gathering. We are to know that the Lord is present. There in the people who gather, in the word that is spoken and the food we receive. Maybe there was a problem in the Johanine community with the Lord's Supper and the author wants to show the community that the Lord is with us in the Eucharistic gathering.

Richard Rohr says of Eucharist, 'You've got to comprehend any great mystery in one focused moment. Great truth must be put on small stages to be able to process and grasp its momentous significance. This is the sacramental principle. believe it, struggle with it, comprehend it here, and then move beyond it and recognise what is true here is true everywhere!'

If we can recognise him then, in elements so ordinary as bread and wine, then maybe we will have the courage to recognise him everywhere else too. Our Eucharistic celebration points us outwards to find the Lord who has 'gone before us into Galilee'. If we can look at bread and wine and say, 'it is the Lord,' then maybe we will be able to look at a brother or a sister and say, 'it is the Lord.'

Within the Catholic tradition we have placed a huge emphasis on the Eucharist and finding the presence of Christ there, and rightly so. Sadly, we often do not make the connections. When we say we believe in the eucharistic presence we are challenged to see that the presence of Christ is everywhere. We are to see it in the stranger and in the friend. We are to recognise him in the outsider and in those who supposedly belong. In short, the challenge of the eucharist is to be like Jesus. He recognised the presence of God everywhere and spent most of his ministry encouraging people to see the presence of God everywhere and not to distinguish between the holy and the unholy.

The last time a charcoal fire is mentioned in the Gospel is when Peter stood warming himself and denied knowing Jesus. At *this* meal Peter is about to be given the chance to undo his threefold denial. 'Peter do you love me.'

There are three different words in Greek that we translate as love. Peter is being invited, as we all are, to go on a journey. The author of the fourth Gospel says that Peter was upset that Jesus asked a third time, 'Do you love me?' It is no wonder. Peter was being asked, in the third question, to give everything for the sake of the Gospel. Of course he was upset. It is decision time for Peter. He says, 'Yes'. In response to that love Jesus says, 'Feed my lambs' and 'Feed my sheep'.

He was to become food for the hungry. He was to become bread broken for the sake of the world. He was to give his life for the Good News. That is the call we are all given. Will we give our lives for the sake of the bigger picture? In terms of this book, will we give our lives for unity?

I recently came across this quotation from a Benedictine monk called Godfrey Diekman He once said, 'What difference does it make if the bread and wine turn into the Body and Blood of Christ and we do not?'

In other words, he was challenging those of us who receive the Eucharist to become bread broken for a better world. We are invited to become those who pour out our lives for the sake of the world, so that we can feed the world with this Jesus who brings life. We are to become love, but the sort of love that rolls up its sleeves and gets dirty and messy. It is only that sort of love that will have an effect in the world and if you cannot love in that way, then words mean little.

I once sat with Sister Helen Prejean who asked me about the work I and others involved on the project to promote spirituality do. As I explained to her how we tried to open the Scriptures for people and give space and opportunity for prayer she kept nodding her head. Eventually she said to me, 'You know Chris, all well and good, and vital, but how do you do show others what that means practically?'

It was then that we began to work with people who have a dementia and their carers. We can speak about love with great eloquence but we are called to be with people in their brokenness and become love. It costs and can be painful but that is the call.

A few months ago I was invited to go and talk to a group of people about the Scriptural understanding of metanoia. They also wanted me to talk about Eucharist. I did not have a clue, but since I had written a book about it I was unable to find a valid reason not to go. While I was there I told them about the first time a woman who lived on the streets kissed me and held me as she cried some of her pain away. Her name was Pam and she stank of stale sweat and alcohol and I did not know what to do in response. She needed human warmth, comfort and to be held. If I appeared to her like a lump of stone she very graciously never said.

That experience challenged me deeply within about transformation. It made me ask the question how real is it in our hearts and minds. It also invited me to reflect on Eucharist and our call to be at one with the least of our brothers and sisters. After the talk a woman came up to me and told me that she was an Anglican

Priest and I waited for her to tell me she had enjoyed the talk. That did not happen. She was horrified that a woman of the streets should have become the means of transformation. She said that even the story had made her flesh creep.

I knew it was a gospel moment, not a comfortable moment but very definitely a Gospel moment. I had a deep certainty that I had come to that place on that night just to tell that woman the story. She said to me that she had been hugely challenged by my understanding of Eucharist and what that might mean for her. She said that she had realised for the first time at a deep level what Eucharist was about and it frightened her as she recognised the need within for deep inner transformation if she was to really serve. All I had done was tell a story!

What that woman realised was that Eucharist draws us deeply into relationship with Jesus and with others. The truth is we need to be transformed to see that clearly. Every time we break the bread we identify with every brother and sister who is broken. Every time we drink from the cup we identify with everyone who shares themselves with another.

Many years ago, when I was training at Ushaw College in Durham, I met a Divine Word Father called Edicio

De La Torre. Ed had been working in the Philippines and had been imprisoned for leading a revolt amongst the people he worked with. Most of them were starving and denied basic human rights. Ed said many challenging things during his stay with us.

One of his most powerful reflections was that we in the West had lost the right to celebrate the Eucharist because we were not on the side of the little ones. Indeed he said we contributed to the poverty. I was quite shocked at the time but while I would not completely agree with him I could understand why he would say such a thing. The bread and wine we share forces us into relationship with our brothers and sisters. It is not some individual devotion that is to makes us feel good. It is the sacrament of unity.

So we are in relationship with every brother and sister. If we are, how can we stand by and let them suffer? How do we walk past the street people and have hard-hearted attitudes to refugees and asylum seekers. Indeed more often than not, we judge the poor and the broken; certainly those on the edges of our own society, in our seemingly sophisticated western world where the success ethic prevails.

Ronald Rolheiser says, 'The Eucharist is a call to move from worship to service, to take the nourishment, the embrace, the kiss we have just received from God and the community and translate it immediately and directly into loving service of others. To take the Eucharist seriously is to begin to wash the feet of others, especially the feet of the poor.

The Eucharist is both an invitation, which invites us, and a grace, which empowers us to service. And what it invites us to do is to replace distrust with hospitality, pride with humility, and self-interest with self-effacement so as to reverse the world's order of things – wherein the rich get served by the poor and where the first priority is always to keep one's pride intact and one's self-interest protected.

The Eucharist invites us to step down from pride, away from self-interest, to turn the mantle of privilege into the apron of service, so as to help reverse the world's order of things wherein pride, status, and self-interest are forever the straws that stir the drink.'

When I read that, I found it so challenging. Most of us, myself included, have made Eucharist a very private reality. Rather than letting it reverse the world's order of things, we have allowed it to become a mirror image of the worlds understanding. We are exclusive rather than inclusive, which naturally gives rise to a sense of superiority and privilege. Self-interest is at the heart

of much of the practice of Eucharist because so
many see it as a means to get into heaven. It has not
freed us to serve but has become a reward for good
moral behaviour. That is why Pope Francis recently
commented that 'The Eucharist, although it is the
fullness of sacramental life, is not a prize for the perfect
but a powerful medicine and nourishment for the weak.'
Have we really learned the lesson?

Yet we are called to serve. Eucharist binds us together.
We cannot celebrate the body of Christ without standing
for those parts of the body that are suffering. That is
why John in chapter thirteen of the fourth Gospel tells
us that it is about getting down on our knees and
washing the feet of our brothers and sisters. It is about
service and becoming the presence of Christ for the
world. Richard Rohr says, 'We keep eating and drinking
the Mystery, until one day it dawns on us in an
undefended moment, My God, I really am what I eat!'

I have written before about the group of women who
meet in our house every Monday. They are strong,
courageous, and faith filled. They share openly and
honestly and at times with a rawness which rends the
heart. Just recently we were celebrating Eucharist and
after we had received, one of them suddenly opened her
eyes and then started to laugh. Soon we were all
laughing with her and when she finally stopped she

said to us, 'Christ lives in me'. The laughter had been the sheer exuberance that had touched her heart and mind at this revelation. One of the other women looked around at us all and said, 'Yes, and what a responsibility that is'. The laughter had given way to a recognition of gift and responsibility to serve the world.

I went to Sunday Mass recently in a Parish in the heart of Liverpool's Vauxhall area, a place poor financially but rich in community values. The Parish Priest is someone I have known for many years. He always has an interesting slant on the Gospel and is very good to listen to. I enjoy being there. There is a huge amount of bustle goes on before Mass as people greet one another and find out what the week has been like. Eventually the celebration began and I enjoyed the sense of community as well as what was shared. When we got to the offertory collection a man in his late thirties got up. It was obviously his job! He wandered up and down the aisle with his basket talking away to himself and occasionally to others. Then a little girl decided to take his job and when the basket came to her she started to hand it around. My friend looked completely bewildered and he began to walk around in circles in the middle of the Church muttering to himself and obviously quite distressed.

In the row behind me were three women. Before Mass

their conversation had kept me entertained as I listened to various health problems which reigned from varicose veins to 'women's problems'. One of these women, it seemed, was moved with compassion. She stood up walked out into the centre of the church, oblivious to other people. She put her arms around the man and in her strong Liverpool accent said, 'C'mon love, you come and sit with us for a while.' She led the man back to her seat and sat next to him still with her arms around him. He began to cry as she held him and kept saying 'I miss her'. The woman was almost crooning as she repeated over and over 'I know, love'. I learned afterwards that his grandmother had died years before, but to him it was though it were yesterday. In moments of stress when he could not cope, it was his grandmother he missed.

At that Eucharistic gathering the unity and service that we are invited into every time we gather to eat and drink was apparent in the gift of an elderly woman to a man who I guess would experience rejection in most places.

So, back to the shores of Galilee and the words to Peter 'Do you love me... then feed my sheep'. He stands there not only for himself but as a symbol of the Church which is invited to feed the world with the presence of Jesus that it has recognised in the breaking of the bread. He stands as a symbol of those who are called to unite the world in the mystery of love through the service of the least of our brothers and sisters. He stands to challenge us all to recognise the invitation to unity that the Eucharist holds out to us.

TWELVE

THE JOURNEY INTO UNITY

My mum's old friend Nellie Roberts often used to talk of her father who was my great grandfather's friend. Like my great grandfather, Nellie's dad had arrived in England from Ireland in the 1880's and settled in Liverpool although his dream had been to go to America. Sadly, the money ran out and no more was forthcoming, hence his staying in Liverpool down by the docks. He made his living from an old cart and horse and would buy and sell anything he could.

Nellie often used to tell the story of one Christmas, when she and her father had responded to the needs of an old Irish woman, who had been widowed some years earlier. Nellie always said she had not wanted to help, but help she had to, and she learnt a valuable lesson.

It was late one Christmas Eve and she was feeling like the world had come to an end because there had not been enough money to buy her the doll that she had wanted for Christmas. She had ranted and raved and cried and screamed but nothing worked. There would be no doll and all Nellie could do was dry her tears and get on with it. Her sisters were not getting their dolls either but they were older than Nellie and accepted their lot.

Nellie and her sisters all had jobs to do and when they had eaten their supper and the washing up was done they settled down in front of the fire to read and sew before bed and get ready for Christmas day. Nellie said that her father was out in the back yard. They thought that he was feeding the horse and getting the cart ready for the next days work. Christmas day or not, he would still have to work.

When her father came back in he looked at Nellie and said. 'Come on, love, get your shawl and bundle up well it's cold out tonight.'

Nellie said that she was really upset then. Not only wasn't she getting the doll for Christmas, now she was being dragged out in the cold.

Outside, it was even worse. In front of the house was the horse and cart ready and waiting. It seemed that whatever it was they were doing, it was going to take some time. Nellie was not happy.

As Nellie looked at the back of the cart she saw that it was full of kindling. She asked her dad what was going on and he simply said 'we are going to see Mrs. Casey.'

Mrs. Casey was a woman who came from the same part of Ireland as Nellie's father. Her husband had died a year or so before and left her with three children, the oldest being eight. Nellie had no idea why they would be going to see her.

Nellie said that he took her by the shoulders and said to her 'I passed by her house today,' and little Billy was outside trying to find some kindling for the fire. Nellie, they've got nothing.' It was then Nellie realised why there was so much wood on the back of the cart. Then Nellie said her dad went into the house and came out with a box. In the box were some clothes and shoes and in a bag some food. They loaded the cart and set off to Mrs Casey's house. She lived in one of the worst slums in Liverpool, in one of the courts off Scotland Road. There were twenty families living in a room each and sharing a toilet that was always overflowing.

Nellie said that they rode in silence and she tried to think through what her dad was doing. They did not have much by worldly standards. So why was her dad giving them food and clothes and shoes they could ill afford to give away?

When they arrived they unloaded the kindling as

quietly as possible and then took the food and clothes to the door. Nellie said that the door opened a crack and there was Mrs Casey. She had a thread-bare blanket wrapped around her. The children were wrapped in another and were sitting in front of a very small fire that hardly gave off any heat at all.

Nellie's dad explained why they had come and how he had seen Billy foraging in earlier in the day. Mrs. Casey bit her lip to keep it from trembling and then tears filled her eyes and spilled down her cheeks. She looked up at Nellie's Dad. She wanted to say something, but it would not come out.

Nellie said that she was not the same person when she went out to help her dad bring the wood in. She had a big lump in her throat and she said that there were tears in her eyes too. Nellie could see that they were literally saving the lives of these people.

Mrs. Casey finally spoke and Nellie said she has never forgotten those words. She said 'God bless you. I know the Lord himself has sent you. The children and I have been praying that he would send one of his angels to spare us.'

At the door, Nellie's dad turned to Mrs. Casey and said, 'You and the children come over for Christmas dinner tomorrow. There will not be much but what we have we will share together. The big surprise was still to come. As they were driving home Nellie's dad told her that he and her mum had been putting away a little money every week in order to buy three dolls but then he had seen Billy looking for wood and knew what he had to spend the money on.

It was then that Nellie understood, and started to cry again. She was so glad that her dad had done what he had done. He had given her a lot more than a doll. He had given her a lesson that would last throughout her life's journey and it was simple. Whatever Nellie Roberts had would be shared with those who did not have enough. She lived that lesson till she was in her nineties.

What we learn on the journey through life is of vital importance. It can be a force for good or bad. The Scriptures are there to help us on our journey into the mystery of God which will always increase our desire for unity and for relationship. If it does not do that then we are not reading and praying the Scriptures in a way that can bring us life. The Bible is a record of people's journey with God. It is a faith story and it is there so that we can see our journey into the mystery, that is God, reflected in it. As we go through the Scriptures, what we see in Israel's growth as a people is a pattern of what happens to every person and to every people who set out on the journey of faith. They go through stages and gradually come to see how God loves them and what God's liberation does for them and also for the whole of humanity. Harmony and integration rather than fragmentation and dis-harmony is the best way for humanity to live.

It is only in walking the journey that we come to know the answers and those answers are not tidy and they are not head answers; they are gut answers. They are meaning and life and they are found in values like love, and compassion, and forgiveness, and oneness.

The Bible was written in faith and can only be understood in faith so I would encourage you to allow the God that this little group of people experienced, to touch your heart and mind and reveal to you the truth that everything belongs together. Discover what it means to be a human being. Discover the joy and the suffering that is part of every human life. Let the stories of an ancient people become your story as they teach you about the journey of humanity which is always the same whatever the period of history. Learn about the call to be one with everything and everybody.

I often hear people talk of the God of the First Testament and the God of the Second Testament as though they were a different species. It is as though God has changed over this period. The vengeful God of the First Testament becomes the loving God of the Second Testament. I think what happens is that people change. God remains. God is the God of steadfast love who never leaves us. Somehow our experience of who God is evolves and grows. It deepens with every passing generation as we move to a deeper level of commitment and vision and understanding.

This is illustrated in the First Testament but the truth is that it is mirrored in our lives as well. The pattern of growth in Israel's faith is the same pattern that we find in anyone's faith life anywhere in the world. It is the universal pattern of faith development which leads us to recognise the pattern that is at the core of everything.

As we begin to recognise the journey in faith I think there are four stages through which faith evolves. It is interesting that all four stages are to be found in the Scriptures. The first three in the First Testament and the fourth in the second. What I would like to try and do is look at these stages of faith in a bit more detail.

We will call the first stage exclusive faith. Abraham and his descendants responded in faith to God's call to believe and trust but the negative side to this was its exclusivity. They thought that God had chosen them to the exclusion of others and their approach eventually became self-righteousness rather than true faith. Everybody else was the enemy. It is the kind of attitude that says she is not Catholic but she is very nice.

I was recently talking to a woman in a local Parish. I had been reflecting on the inclusive nature of Luke's Gospel. Afterwards Agnes came to me. She was a nice ordinary woman who went to Mass every Sunday, sometimes during the week and was a Eucharistic Minister. She began to talk to me about what I had said and at one point when talking about God's unconditional love she said something like, 'that is all well and good but you cannot trust those Moslems, they will cut your heads off.' It was that first stage of faith being shown so clearly.

The characteristics of this type of faith are loyalty to the religious leaders without very much thought of others. Foreign beliefs are seen as threatening and false. Symbols that identify people as chosen are clung to and there is a refusal to be contaminated by ideas and practices which are different. We do not have to go too far back in the church's history to see that we operated from that level of faith for a long time, and despite Vatican II which calls us to growth, still do operate from it in many, many ways.

It is a very limiting stage of faith development because it stops us really responding to the call of the Lord and quite often gets caught up in self-righteousness and religiosity. Loyalty to the group is more important than anything else. It is certainly simpler than trust in God because there is little personal involvement at this level of faith. There is no need to trust and no need to grow. It can be a very comfortable level of faith because we can deal in terms of right and wrong, black and white. I have been told that this level of faith is particularly good for the male psyche. I cannot imagine why! Seriously, to enter into relationship, to have to trust and grow is risky and we would rather not take the risk.

The danger with this sort of faith is that it naturally leads to the belief that since some are chosen, others are not, or since we are loved by God, others are not. This can give us a right to hate or even destroy what God does not love. What happened in Israel's history is that they self-righteously slaughtered those who were not like themselves.

The First Testament is full of stories and battles as the people of Israel took the land that God had promised them. This type of primitive religious morality led Christians to believe that it was justifiable to torture or burn those they called heretics or to believe that killing people in their thousands in the crusades was something God approved of. We need to move on from that stage of faith because of its limitations and obvious dangers and deepen our awareness of what God is calling us to, particularly in the area of unity. Why would we give our lives for the common good if our level of faith is such that we can exclude and separate?

We will call the second stage of faith Covenant faith. In an earlier chapter we reflected on the Exodus story as a means of healing our fragmentation. When the Israelites followed Moses out into the desert they knew they were loved by the God who had set them free from the power of the Egyptians. They were called to a deeper level of faith and responded by entering into a covenant with God. They were not able to recognise at this stage that God's love was infinite and boundless and so they heard God's love being offered to them in terms of an agreement. God's love was always unconditional they were just unable to see that. So God took them where they were and revealed as much as they were capable of understanding.

That sort of faith leads to a tit for tat mentality. God will save us if we obey the commandments and if we do not, then God will punish us. It is all about earning God's love and storing up enough merits to make sure that they outweigh your faults. Catholics have been especially prone to this sort of thinking but really all it does is make what we do the focus, rather than what God does. At this level of faith we are trying to save our souls rather than allowing God to save us.

It is a level of faith that many love to take refuge in. Human beings are not good at unconditional. As I said before we deal in terms of black and white and good and bad. We create cosy little huddles of people who think the same as we do. We judge people and have some who are in and therefore acceptable and some who are out and so intolerable. Yet God is bigger and more than we care to imagine. God does not deal in black and white and in and out. God can be trusted with mess.

We do not have to earn the love of God. It is freely given and does not depend on us. The virtue at this level of faith is that of obedience. It is not all bad, but the danger with it is that it becomes the faith of the Pharisees. It says 'Keep the law and everything will be fine.' It is very self-protective and self-satisfying and it is probably a stage that we all have to go through. However if we are journeying and growing in faith we cannot stay at that level. If we do it simply blocks growth, and there are so many people stuck in this stage, where faith is identified with obeying the commandments and performing the correct rituals in order that God will be pleased with us.

The sort of God that typifies this level of faith is the great policeman in the sky or the Monty Python foot that comes down from heaven. The God who keeps check on people justifying the punishment of those who do wrong. There needs to be movement in faith if we are to see the true God who brings life in its fullness. What does that say about unity? How can we be united with people who do not live in the same way as we do?

My aunty Maureen lived in a row of terraced houses near the centre of Liverpool. She had lived there most of her life and was very well known in the area. She was a Eucharistic Minister at the local Church and very involved in the Legion of Mary. Over the years many of the old neighbours had died or moved away. Apart from a few friends who had stayed, aunty Maureen was becoming more and more isolated. Her next door neighbours were Moslem and aunty Maureen welcomed them. She became firm friends with the family who kept an eye on her. Aunty Maureen loved their children who often popped in to sing her a song or tell her what they had been doing in school. One day I was visiting and her neighbour called in and as she was leaving this lovely woman said to me that aunty Maureen had been the only person in the street to welcome them. She had tears in her eyes when she explained that while they were different and worshipped differently, they had experienced nothing but warmth and welcome at aunty

Maureen's house. Why would you reach out to those who are different if you were not sure of the truth of God's universal love for humanity?

The third stage could be called prophetic faith. The prophets were the first people to realise that Israel's understanding of God was far too limited. The Prophets discovered that God was with them in their suffering as well as in their triumph. They discovered that God still loved them even when they sinned and even when their ritual temple worship fell apart. The prophets began to see everything as grace.

The God of the prophets and the wisdom writers is a God of compassion and mercy, a forgiving and loving God. The Lord loves Israel even though, like Hosea's wife, she prostitutes herself before other Gods. The Lord is patient and remains faithful even when Israel wanders away. When Israel went into exile, the Lord went too and through the prophets promised to lead Israel by the hand and lead her home when her banishment was over.

The image that best captures the prophetic insight into the heart of God is the Isaiah's image of the suffering servant. The God who has been revealing Godself all along is a lover and a servant. The desire of God's heart is to know us, love us, and to serve us.

It is the most incredible truth that goes beyond the intellect and cuts to the very depth of our being and it frightens the life out of us. We have for so long made God in our own image and likeness that we have begun to believe the lie that God is simply a more self righteous version of ourselves. To believe in the power of unconditional love is to blow our minds and shatter our illusions and falsehoods and most of us do not want to do that.

I guess that is why it has taken humanity so long to get a glimpse of. It is also why, when the prophets began to get a glimpse of it, they made God completely other than us. Their insight was incomplete because they still pictured God as out there, beyond the realm of the human, living at a distance. When they thought of salvation they saw the Messiah coming from afar changing the wickedness of the world and setting things right.

Even when we have prophetic faith we can sometimes suffer from the same short-sightedness and wonder why God is not doing more to make people do the right thing. Why cannot God change the hearts of the people who want to maim and hurt others? So we can fail to recognise that we are all children of an unconditionally loving God and therefore every human person is worthy of respect and dignity. When we fail to recognise that truth then unity with every human being becomes a meritocracy. We will be united with those who deserve God's unconditional love not with those who are not deserving.

Many years ago I worked with a wonderful religious sister who brimmed over with God's love. She worked with people who had nothing and her heart was broken for the poor. Her compassion knew no bounds and she was fearless in her defence of those who lived on the streets or who were threatened with eviction from poor housing. She could be found out on the streets with hot soup in the depths of winter. Her community used to spend most of the year knitting scarves, hats, and gloves for the winter ahead and Mary would distribute them on her soup run. However should any of Mary's clients cross her in any way then she would never forget the slight or the hurt that she experienced. While she would never stop ministering to those people there was a sourness about the way she treated them. She would talk about them and her service of them was tainted with suspicion and mistrust. Yes, she would say, God loved them but God should do something to make them more grateful and easier to get on with.

Maybe what happens is that we become blind to recognising that God is giving us the power of the Spirit to redeem the world and draw all men and women into unity. Beyond the faith of the prophets and beyond the faith that God loves us unconditionally is a deeper faith which we only discover in the Second Testament. The final level of faith to which God calls us is that total and unreserved 'Yes' to God's request to be present in and through the world in us. God's unconditional love is to flow through us and into the lives of others. The full redemption of humanity is to occur in us so that the salvation of the world can be brought out through us. It is incarnational faith and those who live at this level have discovered real freedom.

Life lived at this level of faith becomes incredibly simple because we realise that God does not demand great things of us, but only wants to great things in us. It is the invitation to trust and surrender in the way the whole of the Scriptures have been asking of us. Surrender and trust at every step. Trust in God's promise and wait for that promise to be fulfilled in our lives.

Mary lived at the transition from the First Testament to the New Testament and she carries the meaning of faith beyond what it has been for Abraham, the Israelites, and the prophets to what it can be for Christians. At the close of the First Testament and at the threshold of the second, God's promise to Abraham is seeing its fulfilment. Human faith has evolved to the point where God's action in human history can begin to be recognised for what it is. At last God's faithfulness comes fully into human history through the faithfulness of those who trust, forgive, and are merciful. It comes into the world in and through those who are willing to draw people together in a unity that goes beyond religious boundaries, sexual orientation, skin colour, or mental health issues.

There are very few people who I think epitomise that level of faith. I have caught glimpses of it throughout my life wherever there is love, forgiveness, and mercy and when I have seen it, it has been an overwhelming experience that has taken my breath away and brought me up sharply. I once was in a hospital in Tanzania and saw a woman holding a child who was dying. With the pain in her eyes and the tears pouring down her cheeks I presumed she was the child's mother. I later learned she had found the child collapsed on the street. Then out of selfless love she had paid for that child's treatment and stayed with him until he died. It was their common humanity that brought them together and in it and through it I saw the face of God. I have seen it in the love that exists in a L'Arche house where people are respected and given their dignity and no one is considered better than the other. I have seen it in countless acts of kindness that build up humanity rather than destroy our common unity.

So I guess the challenge for us is to ask ourselves where we are on this journey of faith. Is it leading us more fully into the wonder of humanity and increasing our desire for unity? Have we moved towards surrendering to God who will always challenge us to live for the common good or are we still separating and dividing and judging and blaming? Are we willing to let go of our own plans and needs and desires for the sake of unity? Are we willing to let go of our preoccupation with sex and material goods and power and allow ourselves to get to the point when all that matters is the love of God working in us and through us? Will we move into that place of incarnational faith when the only reality that is important is the drawing together of God's people into unity to mirror the reality of the creator? This will bring life to the world and is the ultimate call on the Christian's life. The question for all of us is, how willing are we to go there?

Further copies of this book
are available from

Goodnews Books
Upper Level
St John's Church
296 Sundon Park Road
Luton, Beds, LU3 3AL

01582 571011
www.goodnewsbooks.co.uk
orders@goodnewsbooks.co.uk

and also Fr Chris' other books:

Meta... what?
Love is the Key
Holiness is for Everyone
Forgiveness is for Giving
When Did We Stop Skipping?